STUDENT BRAIN FOOD

D0120574

www.palgravestudyskills – **the leading study skills website**

You may also be interested in the following study titles by Palgrave Macmillan:

14 Days to Exam Success *Lucinda Becker*

Brilliant Writing Tips for Students *Julia Copus*

Cite Them Right (9th edn) *Richard Pears and Graham Shields*

Critical Thinking Skills (2nd edn) *Stella Cottrell*

The Exam Skills Handbook (2nd edn) *Stella Cottrell*

Getting Critical *Kate Williams*

How to Get a First *Michael Tefula*

How to Use Your Reading in Your Essays (2nd edn) *Jeanne Godfrey*

How to Write Better Essays (3rd edn) *Bryan Greetham*

The Palgrave Student Planner *Stella Cottrell*

Planning Your Essay *Janet Godwin*

Reading and Making Notes *Jeanne Godfrey*

Referencing and Understanding Plagiarism *Kate Williams and Jude Carroll*

Reflective Writing *Kate Williams, Mary Woolliams and Jane Spiro*

Report Writing *Michelle Reid*

Skills for Success (2nd edn) *Stella Cottrell*

Studying with Dyslexia *Janet Godwin*

Study Skills Connected *Stella Cottrell and Neil Morris*

The Study Skills Handbook (4th edn) *Stella Cottrell*

Time Management *Kate Williams and Michelle Reid*

The Undergraduate Research Handbook *Gina Wisker*

University Life *Lauren Lucien*

Write it Right (2nd edn) *John Peck and Martin Coyle*

Writing for University *Jeanne Godfrey*

You2Uni *Stella Cottrell*

For a complete listing of all titles in our Study Skills range please visit
www.palgrave.com/studyskills

STUDENT BRAIN FOOD

EAT WELL, STUDY BETTER

Lauren Lucien

palgrave
macmillan

First published 2013 by
PALGRAVE MACMILLAN

Palgrave Macmillan in the UK is an imprint of Macmillan Publishers Limited, registered in England, company number 785998, of Houndmills, Basingstoke, Hampshire RG21 6XS.

Palgrave Macmillan in the US is a division of St Martin's Press LLC, 175 Fifth Avenue, New York, NY 10010.

Palgrave Macmillan is the global academic imprint of the above companies and has companies and representatives throughout the world.

Palgrave® and Macmillan® are registered trademarks in the United States, the United Kingdom, Europe and other countries

ISBN: 978-1-137-29704-4

This book is printed on paper suitable for recycling and made from fully managed and sustained forest sources. Logging, pulping and manufacturing processes are expected to conform to the environmental regulations of the country of origin.

A catalogue record for this book is available from the British Library.

A catalog record for this book is available from the Library of Congress.

Printed and bound in the UK by Charlesworth Press, Wakefield.

For my lovely Grannie, who makes the best
boiled egg and soldiers in the world.

CONTENTS

FOREWORD

How do you get people to eat healthily and enjoy what they eat at the same time?

This is a question that preoccupies those who work in the area of food and nutrition and is unfortunately confused, and thus not helped, by the incomplete, and sometimes incorrect, interpretations of the science, health and well-being associated with this fundamental for life. I do not pretend to have the answers to the question I pose above, and neither does this book. What I do know as someone who enjoys food is that whether it is a magnificent culinary creation that causes one's taste buds to explode or a basic meal provided to simply maintain and sustain us, food, in its preparation as well as in its consumption, can give us joy and comfort; it can bring a moment of peace and clarity when you have a deadline (believe it or not) or when your thoughts are troubled.

How do these words have any relevance to you, the university student, dealing with your new-found independence? Well, hopefully they and this book will help you see food as more than a necessity, something that you have to eat. These simple and mouth-watering recipes, ranging from the humble baked potato to the puff pastry pizza, will form the basis for your creation of a range of simple and healthy meals with which you will impress not only yourself but your friends, family and maybe even a date or two!

Simplicity and being conscious of what we are eating and what it could do for our mind and body are the main themes of this book. It addresses the challenges of shopping and cooking on a budget, an issue that is very apt in these economically austere times, as well as the need to create meals that not only satisfy but help to maintain health and well-being when studying. Please note, and this is where I put my nutritionist's hat on, this book is not a promise that these meals will make you cleverer or boost your memory when you most need it (the night before an exam, for example). It will not ensure that you can stay up all night writing an essay that you have had a month to do, make you more beautiful than you already are or give you shiny hair.

Lauren Lucien, a recent graduate of Kingston University and so someone who knows, understands and has witnessed the challenges of being a student in the twenty-first century, has put together a series of recipes that, with some input from me, should help students appreciate some of the science behind what they eat.

I hope you and your friends will enjoy preparing and consuming many of these recipes – so get cooking!

Dr Elizabeth Opara, BSc (Hons), DPhil, RNutr
Principal Lecturer in Nutrition,
Kingston University, UK

ACKNOWLEDGEMENTS

Thanks to all of my friends and family who allowed me to share their best recipes. Special thanks to Fiona Anderson, Joanna Gough and Kate Oliver for reviewing the book.

Extra thanks to my extremely talented sister Rebecca Miller, who shot the photos so brilliantly. Thanks to Mark Liebenberg for equipment, time and some extra-special shots.

Dr Opara, you have been vital to this project and your advice has been invaluable! Thank you so much for sharing your insider knowledge with us.

Thanks to Suzannah Burywood, Della Oliver and the team at Palgrave Macmillan for making the book look so wonderful.

Also, thanks to Larry for letting us use your kitchen and Liam for allowing me to burn many a pot and keep on trying before I finally learnt how to make perfect basmati rice.

The author and publishers would like to thank Heriot Watt University (copyright holder), by permission of photographer Matt Davies (**www.shashin.co.uk**) for the use of an image on the front cover.

INTRODUCTION

As a student I discovered that there was a direct link between what I ate and my energy and concentration levels when studying. Trying to 'boost' my body and mind with energy drinks just made me feel sick after a while, and I was eating crisps and junk food because of the stress of not being able to revise and write essays in the way I knew I could. Then there was the financial drain – takeaways, snacks from the pasty shop and other fast food was expensive, plus I'd be hungry an hour later because it wasn't a filling or balanced meal.

So with all these things in mind, I started to change my eating and lifestyle habits bit by bit and found that the food I made myself was cheaper and healthier than junk food.

I wrote *Student Brain Food* to help more students save money, eat better and understand *what* they are eating. I teamed up with Dr Opara, Principal Lecturer in Nutrition at Kingston University, London, to bring you an intelligent student cookbook that feeds your body *and* your mind.

Enjoy learning more about nutrition, saving money and of course trying out all the tasty recipes in *Student Brain Food*!

HOW TO USE THIS BOOK

This indicates how many people the meal will serve.

This suggests how long each recipe should take to prepare and cook.

This symbol indicates how much the recipe will cost:

is cheap to make

is moderately cheap to make

is more expensive to make.

These are my suggestions for extra or alternative ingredients that you could use in the recipe (cook them appropriately before adding).

These are my insider tips, tricks and info to help you save money, be your best in the kitchen and eat smarter as a student.

Goes well with: Use the 'Goes well with' boxes to see what side you can add to your meal – or which main dishes go with the side you've chosen.

Dr Opara, Principal Lecturer in Nutrition at Kingston University, shares her insider knowledge and guidance in bubbles like this.

LEMON, GARLIC AND HERB CHICKEN

53

Feeds 4
45 minutes

GRAB

- 2 tablespoons garlic puree
- 2 tablespoons lemon juice
- 2 tablespoons dried mixed herbs
- Pinch of salt
- 6 chicken pieces (thighs or legs), with skin

You can also use the lemon, garlic and herb mixture with chicken breast fillets, fish or even chicken wings.

Goes well with:
Basmati Rice, page 98, Easy Cook Rice, page 98, Three Veg Mash, page CC, Cheesy Chive Potato Bake, page 42

This recipe is great because you get all the flavour without having to marinate the chicken for hours. The garlic adds to the tastiness and it also contains selenium, which is needed to keep the immune system in good working order. This recipe is delicious – great for date night!

EASY EATS

GO

1 Preheat the oven to 150°C/320°F/Gas Mark 2.

2 Warning: this can get a bit messy! In a bowl, mix together the garlic puree, lemon juice, salt and mixed herbs. Use your fingers to carefully pull back the skin from the chicken, then spread a thin layer of the mixture underneath the skin. Fold the skin back over the chicken.

3 Line a baking tray with kitchen foil, place the chicken on it and put in the oven for 30 minutes. *Baste* twice with the juices that run off the chicken. Check the inside of the chicken and make sure that no pink remains and the juices run clear. Leave to rest for a minute then serve.

- 1 teaspoon olive oil

Replace the chicken and bacon with cooked king prawns and a squirt of lemon juice for a lighter version.

DR OPARA'S FOOD FOR THOUGHT
"A junk food lunch will fill you up, but how long until you begin to feel peckish and all you can think about is food and not the book chapter or journal article you have to read to get your head round that assignment?

1
FORWARD THINKING AND PLANNING FOR SUCCESS

YOUR SHOPPING LIST FOR THE WEEKLY FOOD SHOP

- **Fresh:** Milk, eggs, fruit for packed lunches and snacks, vegetables (greens, potatoes, carrots, stir-fry, onions, garlic), cheese, yoghurt, butter, sausages, meat (see also frozen).
- **Dry:** Bread, cereals/oats, noodles/pasta, rice, nuts, stock cubes.
- **Jars/cans/bottles:** Baked beans, tinned tomatoes, tuna, sweetcorn, sugar, olive oil.
- **Frozen:** Meat (chicken, mince, beef, lamb), tofu.

BASIC FOOD HYGIENE

Some quick dos and dont's

- **Do** keep cheese in an airtight container. You can alternatively use a plastic food bag and tie a knot at the top.
- **Do** keep your fridge at 3–5°C to prevent food decay.
- **Do** check the Best Before date on your food. With certain foods this is more to do with quality than whether you can still eat it or not. For example, lettuce may have started to go brown at the edges or fruit may have become soft, but you can still eat it. When it comes to meat and fish, though, stick to the Best Before date – don't risk it!
- **Don't** miss the signs of decay: shrivelling, mould, a bad smell and sliminess.
- **Don't** pick off mould that you can see and then eat the food. For example, in a slice of bread the green mould actually shows the later stage of decay; there may be tiny white mould spores within the bread that you aren't able to see with just a quick look.
- **Don't** use the same chopping board for cutting up meat and preparing vegetables – the mix of bacteria can lead to food poisoning.

Food poisoning

Food poisoning happens when the food you eat has been contaminated. The common symptoms of food poisoning are feeling sick, vomitting, stomach cramps and diarrhoea. These symptoms don't always arise straight away – sometimes they may even show up three days after consuming the food.

Here are five simple ways to avoid food poisoning:

1 Wash your hands thoroughly with hot water and anti-bacterial hand wash or soap. Do this between handling different types of food, like raw meat and vegetables, or after touching a pet or the bin.

2 Use separate chopping boards for meat and vegetables and keep raw meat separate from *everything*, as juices from the meat can contaminate surfaces and other foods.

3 Thaw food in your fridge, not on the side, so that it cannot reach room temperature.

4 Only reheat food once.

5 Avoid eating shellfish or fish that has been left out at room temperature.

According to the HPA (Health Protection Agency), Salmonella bacteria are a frequent cause of food poisoning. Most people recover without treatment after 2–3 days, but if you become seriously ill you may need hospital care because the dehydration (fluid loss) caused by the illness can be life threatening. See www.hpa.org.uk/Topics/InfectiousDiseases/InfectionsAZ/Salmonella/ for more information.

E. coli food poisoning is another common form, particularly after eating meat that is not cooked through properly, for example at a BBQ – so always check before you bite! According the UK National Health Service website, *E. coli* is 'bacteria found in the digestive system of many animals, including humans. Most strains are harmless but some strains can cause serious illness'. See www.nhs.uk/Conditions/Food-poisoning for more information.

The student fridge

Even the way you organise your fridge can prevent food wastage and food poisoning. See the opposite page for how a healthy fridge looks. Notice that the meat is covered and on the bottom shelf, so no juices drip onto any food below. The salads are sealed in a drawer. The dairy is organised and on the top shelf. In this way cross-contamination is avoided.

Reheating, chilling and freezing

This is where it can get tricky, so follow these tried-and-tested tips to make your food last longer and still be safe:

- Whether you're reheating food on the hob, in the oven or, more commonly, in the microwave, make sure it's piping hot before you serve it. Stick a knife in the middle of the food and test it for temperature. If it's warm, cool or cold, it needs to go back in.

- When reheating in a microwave, especially soup, use a microwaveable cover to keep the food from splattering onto the microwave door or interior.
- When storing leftovers or fresh food in the fridge, it's important to use containers with a lid. Clingfilm can be pierced and also it can slip off, leaving your food uncovered. If someone spills something in their section of the fridge, the lid will take it and your food won't become contaminated.
- When sharing a fridge, use small storage boxes with lids to store your vegetables and meat separately. This deters bacteria and keep the freshness sealed in and decay out! If you do get a takeaway, you can save the plastic boxes for storage.
- Once a tin has been opened, it should be rinsed out and thrown into the recycling, not used to store any leftovers in. If you don't have somewhere to recycle it, close the end by pressing down on it with your foot – wearing shoes, of course! If your bin bags are torn open, doing this stops foraging animals from getting their heads caught.
- Cooked rice and pasta are breeding grounds for bacteria. Cool them quickly, keep them in the fridge for up to two days and only reheat once.

- If you have leftovers and you're going to be eating out or at your mates' house, freeze them for another time rather than leaving them in the fridge – you may forget about them.
- Keep your onions, garlic, potatoes and sweet potatoes out of the light. You can store them in a cupboard to avoid them sprouting.
- If you defrost something, do not refreeze it.
- Defrost in the fridge – never leave your food out on the side or in the oven or microwave. This avoids contamination from bacteria or even rodents, and helps stop you getting food poisoning.

'Does this smell OK to you?'

We've all been there – funds are low, stomach is rumbling, essay deadline is looming. You open the fridge and have a rummage, you feel something slimy at the back, you back away…

The number one golden rule is: store leftovers for one day. After that, freeze them until you need them, defrost in the fridge and eat the same day.

Make and eat food with more than one person if you can to avoid wastage. For guidance on following Best Before labels etc., flick to the section on food lingo on page 11.

The best way to avoid food going mouldy is to store it in the right way, as outlined above. However, if something does escape your grasp, follow these guidelines:

- If there's green or white mould on *anything*, chuck it out.
- Throw milk away if it smells sour or is lumpy when poured out. If it's coming close to its use-by date and you're going away or aren't going to use it, you can freeze it.
- Cheese is off when it starts to get mouldy, smells sour or the edges start to toughen up.
- Discard meat when it loses its colour, turns brown in patches or smells strongly.
- Check the stamped date on eggs for freshness. If there's no date, put the egg in a pan of cold water – if it floats it's off.
- Potatoes and sweet potatoes should be thrown away when there are excessive shoots or patches of purple, green or dark brown.
- Get rid of mushrooms when they become slimy and get mould in the cap coupled with dark brown shiny patches.
- Onions should be chucked out if they turn slimy, have mould around the top and bottom or have green shoots.
- Garlic if off if it turns yellow and soft or has long green shoots.

- For fruit and veg in general, when it stops looking and feeling firm, it's off, so look out for:
  - shrivelled or wrinkled skin
  - lack of shine
  - an overly squidgy feel
  - fluffy grey mould inside when you cut it open
  - mould around stalks.
- Discard salad when the leaves go brown around the edges, wilt or lose their crunch, or if the cucumber is slimy and shrivelled.
- Fresh herbs should be thrown away when they loose their shape and shrivel, or are limp and faded.
- If your fridge smells less than fresh, put in half a lemon to neutralise odours.

Clean as you go

As well as following good food hygiene, it's important to keep the kitchen clean. Here are some tips:

- Mop up any spills as quickly as you can. For raw meat juices I always use kitchen roll and throw it away so the problem is gone immediately.
- Sweep and mop the floor regularly to avoid feeding the mice!
- I know it's a drag, but don't leave washing up to pile up – wash as you go or stack in the dishwasher.

- I leave washing up to air dry rather than ending up with a few soaking wet tea towels. If you do use tea towels, wash them every time you or your housemates do a clothes wash to keep them clean.
- Use disposable kitchen towel rather than a dish cloth to avoid spreading bacteria from place to place.
- Heat kitchen sponges in the microwave for a few seconds to kill off bacteria.

DR OPARA'S FOOD FOR THOUGHT
If you wish to compare brands based on their nutritional content then check the nutrition labels on the front, back or side of the products.

2
TOOLS OF THE TRADE

UTENSILS

- Slatted ladle – used for picking up pasta, turning salad, removing poached eggs from the pan.
- Ladle – used for stirring, pouring sauces over meat.
- Long wooden spoon – doesn't scratch the pan, used for stirring hot sauces, soup and food that is in a deeper saucepan.

- Slatted turner – used to flip eggs, pancakes, pick up fish from the pan.
- Small wooden spoon – doesn't scratch the pan, good for stirring and tasting with, used for beating cake mixture.
- Masher – for when a fork just isn't enough! Good for potatoes, root vegetables and even fruit.

- Balloon whisk – good for whisking pancake batter, cake mix and stirring sauces.

POTS AND PANS

- Frying pan – for eggs, meat, onion, garlic and small meals.
- Saucepan – for making and reheating sauces, poaching eggs, making small portions of pasta or rice.
- Deep saucepan – for recipes that include cooking with three or more ingredients, like Chilli Con Carne (see page 144) or Easy Spag Bol (see page 50).
- Wok – great for cooking thin slices of vegetables or meat quickly, like in You Choose Stir Fry (see page 70).
- Three-tier steamer – genius! Cook your potatoes in the bottom, fish in the middle and veggies on top.
- Lidded cooking pot – for making soups, or for larger portions of rice or pasta.

YOU'LL ALSO NEED...

- Sharp knives for chopping and dicing
- Chopping boards – one for meat, one for vegetables and fruit
- Tablespoons
- Teaspoons
- Fork
- Pint glass
- Mug
- Peeler
- Designated kitchen scissors – very handy for cutting up pizza or loose herbs, opening packaging etc
- Can opener
- Tea towels
- Washing-up sponges
- Kitchen roll
- Plates and bowls
- A large bowl for mixing
- Plastic containers for storing and freezing food
- An apron to save on laundry
- Oven gloves

ESSENTIAL STUDENT STAPLES

Cupboard must-haves

- Bread
- Rice
- Pasta
- Noodles
- Stock cubes
- Cereal
- Baked beans
- Kidney beans
- Soy sauce
- Olive oil
- Seasonings – salt, pepper, chilli flakes, mixed herbs etc
- Pesto
- Teas
- Sugar
- Onions
- Garlic
- Potatoes

Fridge must-haves

- Butter
- Eggs
- Milk
- Cheese
- Mayonnaise
- Vegetables
- Salad
- Ketchup

Freezer must-haves

- Extra bread
- Puff pastry for quick pizzas
- Milk in plastic bottles
- Meat
- Frozen vegetables

3
USEFUL INFORMATION

Food lingo

Here are explanations for some of the terms used in the book that you may not have heard before. In the recipes I've put them in italics, so check back here if you need more information when you're cooking.

- *Al dente* – an Italian term that suggests that food should be firm and have a slight bite to it. Usually applied to pasta.
- *Baste* – pour the juices from the food back over it to keep it moist.
- *Beat* – stir vigorously.
- *Brown* – fry meat quickly just on the outside to seal in flavour and add colour before stewing.
- *Cream* – beat until light and fluffy, usually with an electric whisk.
- *Cube* – chop into small cubes (also dice).
- *Crush* – use the back of a knife or a garlic crusher to break down, usually garlic.
- *Dice* – see cube.
- *Drizzle* – scatter oil or a dressing over something.
- *Florets* – the parts of a broccoli or cauliflower that are not stalk.
- *Fold* – blend lighter and heavier ingredients by folding them into each other gently.
- *Knead* – Fold and press dough by hand.
- *Marinate* – coat food, typically meat, in a glaze or sauce, for a specific length of time to add flavour and softness.
- *Omega 3* – Omega 3 fats are essential to keep yourself in good health. They help to reduce heart disease and are vital for brain function and cell membrane maintenance. Omega 3 fats are found in oily fish like crab, tuna and salmon, but can also be found in smaller quantities in pumpkin seeds and even soya beans.
- *Poach* – gently *simmer* food in liquid, generally milk, stock or wine.
- *Reduce* – rapidly boil liquid in a pan to about half the quantity, resulting in a thicker sauce.
- *Roast* – cook meat or vegetables in an oven for a longer time to keep it tender and juicy.

- *Sauté* – cooking food in fat over a high heat, tossing the ingredient.
- *Score* – use a knife to make small, shallow cuts.
- *Simmer* – to allow the food or liquid to stay just below boiling point.
- *Steam* – cook over boiling water by use of steam, in a three-tier steamer for example.

Handy conversions

°C	°F	Gas Mark	Effect	Fan Oven °C
110°	225°	¼	Very slow/low	90°
120°	250°	½	Very slow/low	100°
140°	275°	1	Slow/Low	120°
150°	300°	2	Slow/Low	130°
160°	325°	3	Moderately slow/Warm	140°
180°	350°	4	Moderate/Medium	160°
190°	375°	5	Moderate/Moderately hot	170°
200°	400°	6	Moderately hot	180°
220°	425°	7	Hot	200°
230°	450°	8	Hot/Very hot	210°
250°	475°	9	Very hot	230°

BE PREPARED

This section includes some basic instructions for preparing and cooking basic ingredients.

Onions

I Chop one end off the onion, leaving the other end on.

2 Peel off the outer layer of the onion.

3 Make vertical slices into the onion towards the remaining end. Then make horizontal cuts across the vertical ones, creating a grid effect.

Garlic

I Using the back of a knife, crush the garlic clove and remove the skin.

2 Slice the clove horizontally into thin ovals.

3 Positioning the knife as in the photo, chop across the slices, sweeping and repeating until the garlic is chopped finely.

Root vegetables

I Chop the ends off the vegetable and peel it.

2 To make into strips, chop the vegetable in half to make two smaller pieces. Now cut into long strips vertically with a sharp knife – be careful.

3 To make into disks, slice the vegetable horizontally.

Peppers

I Cut off the stalk end of the pepper.

2 Remove the stalk in the middle and the seeds.

3 Chop vertically into 3–4 pieces.

4 Slice the pieces vertically to make strips, then line up and cut the strips horizontally to make small squares.

Rice

1 Use about a cup of rice and two cups of water for long-grain and easy-cook rice. If in doubt, follow the instructions on the back of the packet.

2 For basmati rice, put the rice in a pan and swirl water around, drain and then repeat until the water runs clear. This washes off the excess starch and stops the grains sticking together. Cook over a low heat with the lid on until the rice is fluffy.

3 Brown rice needs to be cooked for longer. The method is the same as long grain, but follow the instructions on the back of the packet for the best outcome.

Pasta

1 I normally use a handful of pasta shapes per person, or for spaghetti a small fist-full of strands.

2 Cook the pasta in boiling water for 3–5 minutes, then test to see how firm it is – keep cooking until it's to your liking. Check the packet for the recommended cooking time.

3 Don't turn the heat up too high, otherwise the water will boil over and the pasta will stick to the pan.

4 You can add a teaspoon of olive oil to the water to stop the pasta sticking together.

4

GET COOKING!

BREAKFAST BITES

BOILED EGG AND SOLDIERS

GRAB

- 1 or 2 eggs
- 1 or 2 slices wholemeal toast
- Butter

Feeds 1
Less than
10 minutes

GO

1 Fill a small pan half full with cold water. Place it over a high heat and bring it to the boil. You'll know that water is starting to boil when bubbles start forming and rising to the surface.

2 Place an egg on a tablespoon and lower it into the water. Put both eggs in at the same time if you're having two. Leave to *simmer* for 3 minutes for a soft-boiled egg (runny), 4–5 minutes for a 'softy-hard' (that's how I like it!) or leave for about 10 minutes for a very hard-boiled egg.

3 Toast and butter your bread and cut into strips. Pile the 'soldiers' up on your plate. Remove the egg(s) from the pan and place in an egg cup. Cut the top off with a knife, then dunk your soldiers in. Don't forget to scoop out the egg from the top!

My Grannie used to make this for me and I still love it just as much. Eggs are so beneficial for us students - they are very low in calories and an amazing source of protein, which gives us energy for those long study days.

FRUIT POTS

Feeds 1
5-10 mins

If you're on the go, make these fruit pots the night before and store in the fridge. The fruit gives you an energy boost in the morning and helps you start with at least three of your five a day. Fruit pots are a really good alternative to sugary breakfast cereals, and are a great refresher after a night of clubbing.

GRAB

3 or more from the list below:

- 6 grapes
- 1 tangerine or satsuma, peeled and segmented
- 4 strawberries, hulled
- ½ apple, sliced
- 1 handful *cubed* pineapple or ½ can pineapple chunks
- ¼ ripe mango, peeled and sliced
- 1 kiwi, peeled and sliced
- ½ banana, peeled and sliced
- 2 tablespoons pomegranate seeds
- 6 raspberries or blackberries
- ½ pear, sliced
- 8 blueberries
- 1 slice watermelon, peeled and chopped
- ¼ cantaloupe melon, peeled and chopped
- 6 cherries (can be pricey!)

GO

1 Peel, core, chop and *cube* your fruit where necessary.

2 Put into a container with a tight-fitting lid – don't forget to bring a fork or spoon!

Serve with a small pot of granola and plain yoghurt to mix into the fruit pot to help you feel fuller for longer.

BREAKFAST BITES

FULL ENGLISH BREAKFAST

Feeds 1
15 mins

GRAB

- 1 tomato, chopped in half
- 2 mushrooms, sliced
- 1 egg
- 1–2 sausages
- 2 rashers of bacon
- Olive oil
- ½ can baked beans

If you don't like beans, you could use spaghetti hoops instead. Serve with buttered toast and ketchup or brown sauce.

GO

1 Put the oven on a low heat and the grill on a medium heat. Place the chopped tomato and sliced mushroom under the grill.

2 In a frying pan, cook the sausages and bacon in a splash of olive oil, on a medium heat, until the bacon is crispy and the sausages are brown on the outside and no pink remains inside. If you're using a non-stick pan, you don't need to add any oil. Slice the sausages down the middle and flatten them if you're in a rush – or just really hungry – as they cook quicker. Remove from the heat once cooked through.

3 Now put the beans into a small pan over a low heat. Bring them to the boil then leave to *simmer* for 3 minutes.

4 Remove the mushrooms and tomato from the grill, then put them with the bacon and sausages onto a plate to stay warm in the oven. Turn off the grill, heat the frying pan again with a dash of olive oil and add the egg. Fry to your taste, hard or soft. Flip once if you like. Add to the warmed plate and serve.

The cooked breakfast is touted as a great hangover cure, although I can't say how true that is. It's very indulgent, so should be eaten perhaps once a month rather than every weekend. You do get your protein, carbs and some vegetables, but try to grill rather than fry to reduce the amount of fat you take in.

DR OPARA'S FOOD FOR THOUGHT
Let's begin with breakfast: this meal is a
must - it should do more than give you a sugar
rush and caffeine boost. It should prepare you both
mentally and physically for a three-hour lecture
or practical that starts at 9am and needs to
keep you going until lunch.

PANCAKES

Feeds 3
15 mins

GRAB

- 5 heaped tablespoons plain flour
- 2 eggs
- ½ pint milk (use a pint glass and fill half full)
- Pinch of salt
- Olive oil

GO

I   Place the flour in a large bowl and make a well in the middle, scooping the flour out with a tablespoon.

2   Crack the eggs into the well, allowing them to fill it up, and add the salt. Whisk the eggs, gradually mixing in the flour and adding the milk a little at a time. Whisk until smooth, then leave the batter to stand for about 15 minutes.

3 Heat a splash of oil in a non-stick frying pan. When the oil begins to smoke, add about 3 tablespoons of the batter and swirl round until the base of the pan is covered.

4 Cook the pancake until the edges start to crisp up and then gently use a spatula to lift up one edge. If the pancake comes away easily, it's time to flip it over and cook on the other side. When fully cooked, place on a plate and cover with a tea towel to keep warm.

5 Repeat until all the mixture is used up.

Impress your friends by making Mickey Mouse pancakes – put a tablespoon of batter in the pan, then add another one opposite. These are the ears. Swirl another tablespoon of mixture so that it joins the two together and forms Mickey Mouse's head. Voilà!

Serve with any of the following: fresh fruit, lemon juice, chocolate spread, sugar, honey or maple syrup.

Pancakes are quick to make and a real treat – maybe for when you've got the grade you need. Using skimmed milk instead of whole milk to make your pancakes can reduce the fat content. For sweetening, honey and maple syrup aren't refined and have extra nutrients that sugar doesn't, so why not give them a try!

POACHED EGGS

Feeds 1
5 minutes

GRAB

- 1 egg
- Salt
- 1 teaspoon malt vinegar or white vinegar (this helps the egg white set and doesn't affect the flavour!)

Serve with hot buttered toast and a dash of Worcester sauce or brown sauce.

The smaller the pan the better for this recipe. Poached eggs are better for you than fried eggs because they aren't cooked in oil or fat. This makes a healthy snack to help you get energised for the day ahead.

GO

1 Fill a small saucepan half full with water. Put in ½ teaspoon salt and 1 teaspoon vinegar. Bring the water to the boil, then turn the heat down until the water isn't *simmering* or moving but is still very hot.

2 Break the egg into a small cup or glass. Get the cup as close to the water in the pan as you can and gently tip the egg out into the water.

3 Now leave the egg to cook. Don't touch anything or move the pan! Stay away for about 2–3 minutes, then come back and check the egg – if the egg white has set then it's ready to eat. Remove the egg with a slotted spatula.

PORRIDGE

Porridge is warm, comforting and really keeps you going, especially on a winter's day. Oats contain slow-release carbs, so starting your day with porridge will help you to stay energised in morning lectures. Add blueberries to provide more nutrients and add flavour.

Feeds 1
10 mins

You can add a teaspoon of nutmeg, cinnamon and honey to make a sweeter porridge. Add half a teaspoon of salt for a savoury version.

GRAB

- 1 mug porridge oats
- ½ mug muesli
- 4½ mugs semi-skimmed milk
- Handful blueberries/ raisins/cranberries or dates/tablespoon cocoa powder (as desired)

GO

1 Pour the oats and muesli into a medium saucepan. Add 4½ mugs of semi-skimmed milk.

2 Stir gently over a medium heat until the porridge starts to bubble. Turn the heat down and let *simmer* for 4 minutes, stirring occasionally. Add any spices or fruit and serve immediately.

SCRAMBLED EGGS

Quick, nutritious and easy to make- a perfect student breakfast! Make sure you add enough fat to the pan, otherwise the eggs will stick and the pan will be a pain to wash up.

GRAB

- 1 teaspoon butter
- 2 eggs
- Salt and pepper
- 1 tablespoon milk (optional)

Feeds 1
5 mins

You can grate cheese on top of the eggs to make a gooey, tasty snack. Serve with toast or bread and butter.

GO

1 Put the butter into a small pan and heat until sizzling. Break two eggs into the pan and sprinkle on some salt and pepper, then add a little milk if you like.

2 Using a wooden spoon or plastic spatula, stir the eggs rapidly so that they break up and 'scramble'. When you can see no more liquid, the eggs are ready. Eat immediately.

YOU CHOOSE OMELETTE

GRAB

- 3 eggs
- 1 teaspoon olive oil
- Salt and black pepper
- Optional fillings: grated cheese, red onion, garlic and herbs, sliced tomato, cooked crispy bacon, cooked spinach, cooked mushrooms, cream cheese, sliced peppers, cooked chicken, ham.

Feeds 1
15 minutes

GO

1 Break the eggs into a mug and *beat* them with a fork. Season with salt and pepper.

2 Heat the oil in a frying pan until it forms tiny bubbles.

3 Add the egg mixture and swirl, covering the base of the pan. Use a spatula to lift the setting side of the omelette and let the gooey egg take its place.

4 Remove from the pan when set, put on a plate and add your choice of fillings to one side of the omelette. Flip the empty side on top of the filled one, press lightly with the spatula and eat!

BREAKFAST BITES

Eggs are a simple, easy snack and quite cheap too. They contain vitamins B1 and B2, which can help to keep your cells healthy. If you're deficient in these vitamins you can become lethargic, so a quick omelette is a great energy booster.

EASY EATS

BAKED POTATO

GRAB

Feeds 1
120 minutes

- 1 large baking potato
- 1 tablespoon olive oil
- Salt and pepper
- Optional fillings: warm baked beans, grated cheese, sour cream mixed with chopped fresh chives, tuna mixed with sweetcorn, grated mature cheddar and finely chopped red onion.

GO

1 Preheat the oven to 180°C/350°F/Gas Mark 4. Pierce the potato several times, rub on some olive oil, salt and pepper, then place in the oven. No need for a baking tray, just place the potato onto the middle shelf.

2 Leave to cook for about an hour and a half. Check after an hour to see how crisp the skin is — if it's still quite soft then it will need another 20 minutes or so.

3 When the potato is fully baked, remove from the oven carefully, as it will be piping hot. Slice an X onto the top of the potato and prise the halves apart. Add your chosen filling and enjoy.

If you're in a hurry, you can cook the potato on high in the microwave. Pierce the potato several times with a fork and cook on maximum power for three minutes, carefully turn it over, then cook on maximum power for another three minutes. Slice down the middle, add your filling and tuck in.

 Goes well with: All-in Salad, page 93

One medium baked potato contains iron, magnesium, potassium, phosphorus and let's not leave out vitamins B1, B3 and B6. In short, baked potatoes are healthy, tasty snacks for the hungry, tired and studying student. Also, the vitamin C in white potatoes acts as an antioxidant that can help to protect your immune system – great comfort food for combating fresher's flu!

EASY EATS

BAKED SWEET CHILLI SALMON

Salmon is a really good source of Omega 3 fatty acids. Red chilli is also a good source of vitamin C, great if you're feeling a bit under the weather or have run out of oranges! Although salmon can be expensive, you can club together and buy a big fresh piece between a few friends - it's often cheaper than buying single fillets.

Feeds 2
50 minutes (+ overnight
marinating)

GRAB

- 2 salmon fillets
- 2 tablespoons sweet chilli sauce
- Salt and pepper (½ teaspoon each)
- Small handful fresh parsley, finely chopped
- 2 cloves garlic, peeled and finely chopped
- 1 teaspoon olive oil
- Juice of 1 lemon

GO

1 Put the olive oil, chilli sauce, salt and pepper in a large ovenproof dish – I usually use a glass lasagne dish. Add the chopped garlic and parsley to the dish along with the juice from the lemon. Mix together.

2 Put the salmon into the dish and gently turn so that the fillets are covered in the marinade. Cover the top with a lid or clingfilm. Leave overnight in the fridge to intensify the flavours and allow the salmon to soak up the marinade.

3 Preheat the oven to 180°C/350°F/Gas Mark 4. Place each salmon fillet on a large piece of kitchen foil. Fold the foil up around the fillet so you make a small parcel. Pour the remaining marinade over the salmon and close up the parcel so the salmon is covered completely and no marinade can leak out.

4 Place the parcels directly onto the oven shelf and bake for 35–40 minutes. Check that the salmon is pink throughout and not dark in the middle. Serve immediately.

Goes well with: New Potatoes, page 109,
Easy Cook Rice, page 98,
Show-Off Rice, page 114

EASY EATS

BEST BBQ WINGS

Feeds 4
50 minutes (+ marinating time)

GRAB

- 1 large pack of chicken wings
- 1 tablespoon clear honey
- 10 tablespoons BBQ sauce
- 1 tablespoon soy sauce
- 1 teaspoon ketchup
- A pinch of black pepper
- ½ teaspoon sugar

GO

1 Mix together all the ingredients other than the chicken. Place the uncooked chicken wings into a bowl and pour the marinade over them. Mix until the wings are covered in the sauce.

2 Leave to *marinate* in the fridge, overnight if possible. The longer you leave them, the better the flavour!

3 Line a large ovenproof dish or deep baking tray with kitchen foil. Place the *marinated* wings onto the tray and place in a preheated oven at 150°/300°F/Gas Mark 2. Bake for about 40 minutes, turning once and *basting* with the sauce throughout.

4 Test the chicken wings to see if they're cooked through by slicing the fleshiest part open with a knife – no pink should remain.

 Goes well with: All-in Salad, page 93, Homemade Garlic Bread, page 106, Spicy Potato Wedges, page 118, Baked Macaroni Cheese, page 96

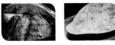

Chicken contains vitamin B3, which helps to regulate the way your body burns fat. Keep your chicken wings lower in fat by removing the skin and baking them (rather than frying) - they're just as tasty! These wings are great for picnics and packed lunches - they taste just as good cold. You can also use this marinade with chicken drumsticks.

BITE-SIZED BANGERS AND MASH

Feeds 4
25 minutes

GRAB

- 2 teaspoons olive oil
- 8 sausages
- 1 onion, chopped finely
- Salt and black pepper
- Gravy granules
- Leftover Black Pepper Mash (or make fresh from recipe on page 100)

You can use different varieties of sausage like apple and pork, Cumberland or the South African sausage Boerewors. Add a splash of red wine to enhance the flavour of the gravy.

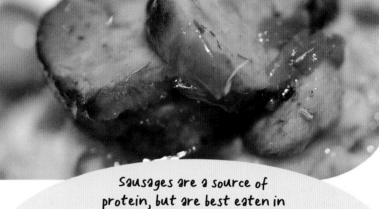

Sausages are a source of protein, but are best eaten in small quantities, as they are often made from processed meat. Try and fork out the extra pound to get a higher meat content in your sausages, as this will reduce your intake of fillers and fats. This recipe is a great stand-by for impromptu study sessions, as it's so quick and simple to make.

GO

1 Put a non-stick frying pan over a medium heat and add the oil. Add the sausages to the pan.

2 Cook the sausages for about 10-12 minutes on a medium heat (reduce the cooking time if the sausages are thin), turning until all the sides are deep brown. Add the chopped onion after about 7 minutes and cook alongside the sausages. Cut the sausages in half and check that no pink remains, then chop into bite-sized pieces.

3 Make gravy by following the directions on the packaging. Serve with the Black Pepper Mash.

BROCCIFLOWER CHEESE

Feeds 2
20 minutes

Broccoli contains high amounts of vitamin K and calcium – great for helping to keep your bones strong. This is good for students since we spend so much time at the computer and tend to slouch. This dish is also extremely cheap to make!

GRAB

- Half a broccoli head, chopped into *florets*
- Half a cauliflower, chopped into *florets*
- White Sauce (recipe on page 91)
- 200g/1–2 handfuls medium or mature Cheddar cheese, grated

GO

1 Fill the bottom pan of a three-tier steamer three-quarters full with water and bring to the boil. Place the second pan on top and layer in the florets of broccoli and cauliflower, place the lid on and *steam* for 6 minutes or until soft. Alternatively, boil the vegetables in a pan of water. Put the *florets* into a sieve or colander to drain and set aside.

2 Prepare the white sauce.

3 Remove the sauce from the heat and quickly stir in the grated cheese until it is completely melted. Stir in the florets and serve as a side or main course.

For a crispy topping, you can also put the white sauce and florets into an ovenproof dish, top with grated cheese and bake in the oven at 200°C/400°F/Gas Mark 6 for 15 minutes.

Goes well with:
Roast Chicken, page 156

CECILIA'S NORWEGIAN STACKERS

Feeds 4
20 minutes

GRAB

- 4 bell peppers (your colour choice), deseeded and sliced into 4 disks
- 4 medium eggs
- 1 pack bread rolls or 8 slices bread
- 2 tablespoons butter
- Handful of salad leaves
- 1 pack smoked salmon
- Salt and pepper

The egg yolk provides half of the egg's total protein, as well as lots of minerals and vitamins. The peppers also contain a good dose of immunity-boosting vitamins A and C. Eat this dish in between study breaks to help you stay energised. It's light and easy to make.

GO

1 Place the pepper slices in a frying pan over a medium heat. Crack an egg into each of the slices. Fry over a medium heat until the eggs are cooked and the pepper has softened.

2 Slice and toast the rolls or bread before spreading butter on each half. Wash the salad leaves and put a large amount on each of the halves, followed by smoked salmon on top.

3 Rest the eggs-in-peppers on top of the smoked salmon and sprinkle over some salt and pepper – enjoy.

Goes well with: All-in Salad, page 93

CHARLOTTE'S CHEAP AND CHEERFUL SAUSAGE PASTA

Feeds 2
30 minutes

GRAB

- 6 sausages
- Olive oil
- 2 cloves of garlic, chopped
- 1 onion, chopped
- Handful of spinach, chopped
- 2 handfuls of pasta shapes
- 1 tin chopped tomatoes
- Squeeze of tomato ketchup

You can use spaghetti instead of pasta shapes or add a topping of parmesan cheese to make it extra tasty.

Add a handful of spinach to this dish to make it extra nutritious. Spinach is one of the best sources of iron, which helps to increase the amount of oxygen in your blood and can help your body operate more efficiently - especially useful when you're taking part in events, campaigns or sports during uni.

GO

I Cook the sausages in a frying pan with a splash of olive oil for about 10–12 minutes (reduce the cooking time for thinner sausages) or until cooked through. Test by cutting one in half – there shouldn't be any pink meat in sight.

2 Remove the cooked sausages and chop them up, then put back in the pan. Add the chopped garlic, onion and spinach and fry for 3–4 minutes.

3 Put the pasta in a pan of boiling water and leave to cook until *al dente*. Drain and set aside.

4 Pour the tomatoes over the sausages, garlic and onions in the pan. Add a squeeze of tomato ketchup for extra flavour. *Simmer* for 5 minutes, then stir into the pasta, serve and enjoy!

 Goes well with: Homemade Garlic Bread, page 106

EASY EATS

CHEESY CHIVE POTATO BAKE

Feeds 2
45 minutes

Use this bake as a side to a roast dinner instead of roast potatoes.

GRAB

- 3 large peeled potatoes, sliced thinly
- 1 clove of garlic, chopped
- 1 red onion, chopped
- 1 tablespoon fresh chives, finely chopped (or use dried)
- 2 tablespoons milk
- 2 tablespoons butter
- 1 large handful grated cheese

GO

1 Preheat the oven to 140°C/275°F/Gas Mark 1.

2 Fill a medium saucepan halfway with water, bring to the boil over a high heat, then add the sliced potatoes. Boil until the potatoes are easy to pierce with a knife. Then turn down the heat so the mixture is *simmering*.

3 Add the chopped garlic, onion, chives and milk into the pan. Allow to *simmer* for another 4 minutes.

4 Over the sink, drain off the liquid from the saucepan using a sieve or colander. Spoon the potato mixture into a large ovenproof dish, three layers high. Dot each layer with butter and sprinkle on some of the cheese. Sprinkle the rest of the cheese on the top.

5 Turn the oven up to 190°C/375°F/Gas Mark 5 and bake for about 40 minutes or until the cheese is golden on top.

Goes well with: Roast Chicken, page 156, Honey Apple Chops, page 140, Lemon, Garlic and Herb Chicken, page 53

Tangy chives are often overlooked, but did you know they are high in Vitamin C as well as quite a few other nutrients and vitamins? Vitamin C is essential for helping to boost your immune system, so why not add some chives to your next salad? When you cook with cheese, try using mature cheddar - you need less than mild or medium to add flavour so your cheese lasts longer.

CHEESY TOMATO BAKE

Feeds 2
35 minutes

GRAB

- 3 handfuls of pasta shapes
- 1 onion, chopped
- Olive oil
- 4 tomatoes, chopped, or a can of tinned tomatoes
- 2 tablespoons tomato puree
- 1 tablespoon ketchup
- 1 teaspoon dried mixed herbs
- Salt and black pepper
- 1 handful grated cheese

Add cooked lean mince, tuna or leftover cooked chicken for a more protein-based dinner, or diced cooked aubergines and red peppers for an alternative veggie version.

`GO`

I Preheat the oven to 190°C/375°F/Gas Mark 5.

2 Bring a pan of cold water to the boil and add the pasta. Boil for 3 minutes and then leave to *simmer* for another 5 minutes, drain and set aside.

3 Put the chopped onion into the same pan and cook in a splash of olive oil until soft. Then chop the tomatoes if fresh and add. Stir in the tomato puree, ketchup, mixed herbs and salt and pepper. Taste and add more seasoning if you like.

4 Put into an ovenproof dish and sprinkle an even layer of cheese over the top. Bake in the oven until the cheese is golden.

Goes well with: All-in Salad, page 93, Homemade Garlic Bread, page 106

If eaten as part of a balanced diet, cheese can be a good source of calcium, magnesium and protein (all of which help to maintain your muscles), and fresh tomatoes are full of antioxidants. Increasing your intake of fruit and veg as part of your diet is a much better way to sustain you throughout your studies than stocking up on things like high-caffeine energy drinks.

EASY EATS

CHICKEN, BACON AND MUSHROOM CREAMY PASTA

GRAB

- 1 handful pasta
- 3 small mushrooms, chopped
- 1 rasher of bacon, chopped
- Teaspoon olive oil
- 3 strips of leftover roast chicken, chopped
- 1 serving White Sauce (recipe on page 91)
- Salt and black pepper

Feeds 1
20 minutes

GO

1 Fill a small saucepan half full with water and bring to the boil, then add the pasta.

2 Chop up the mushrooms and bacon into small pieces and place in a medium frying pan. *Drizzle* with a little olive oil and fry gently until the mushrooms are cooked through and the bacon begins to crisp. Now add the roast chicken and cook thoroughly for 10 minutes until it is heated through.

3 When the pasta is cooked, drain and put back in the saucepan. Pour over the white sauce and add the bacon, chicken and mushrooms. Stir and season with salt and pepper to taste.

4 You can make this into a bake by doubling the ingredients, placing in an ovenproof dish and covering with grated cheese. Bake at 150°C/300°F/Gas Mark 2 until the cheese is golden brown.

This is still one of my favourite recipes. Using a little bit of bacon adds flavour to the dish and is better than overseasoning with salt. Since bacon can be quite fatty, enjoy it as a treat rather than consuming it on a regular basis. You can use up leftovers in this recipe (like cooked chicken), and can even use leftover noodles instead of the pasta.

CHICKEN PESTO PASTA

Feeds 2
30 minutes

GRAB

- 1 handful spaghetti or linguine
- 1 handful cooked chicken, stripped from the bone, or two cooked chicken fillets
- 2 tablespoons pesto
- 1 teaspoon lemon juice

Try using red pesto for a more savoury, tangy taste.

GO

1 Bring a large pan of water to the boil and add the pasta. Boil for about 4 minutes, then turn down to *simmer* until the pasta is *al dente.* Drain and put to one side in a bowl.

2 Tear off small strips of the cooked chicken and stir into the pasta. Add the pesto and a squirt of lemon juice.

Pesto is normally made of basil leaves, olive oil and pine nuts. The basil leaves contain vitamin C – essential for maintaining your immune system. This is a really filling and comforting recipe during the winter.

DEEP-FILL SANDWICHES

Feeds as many as you need!
10 minutes

GRAB

- Bread
- Butter
- Fillings of your choice – try any of these:
- Leftover sliced chicken breast, chopped red onion, mayonnaise and tinned sweetcorn
- Cooked and sliced bacon, lettuce, tomato and mayonnaise
- Hard-boiled egg mashed with 1 tablespoon mayonnaise
- Sliced cheese, sliced red onion and pickle
- Shredded cooked chicken, cooked couscous, sliced tomato and sliced cucumber
- Cooked couscous, chopped red pepper and chopped red onion
- Cooked and sliced bacon, grated cheese and pickle
- Grated cheddar and sliced salami
- Shredded cooked chicken, grated cheese, lettuce and mayonnaise
- Tinned tuna mixed with mayonnaise
- Cooked prawns mixed with mayonnaise and black pepper
- Grated cheddar
- Sliced ham, sliced tomato and DIY coleslaw (see recipe on page 103)
- All American peanut butter and jam
- Leftover avocado, chicken & bacon salad (see recipe on page 94)

Leftovers from the weekend are very handy for making sandwiches for Monday!

GO

1 Butter the bread and add the filling of your choice.

2 Wrap in clingfilm and add to your bag to eat when you're hungry!

Can't wait for your student loan to arrive? Make your own sandwiches instead of paying for them to help save those last few pennies. Try to mix and match your bread. Use white if you really like it, but mix it up with wholemeal, granary or even rolls. If you feel bloated when you sit down to study after eating bread, try rye bread, easily found in most supermarkets, or gluten-free bread.

EASY EATS

EASY SPAG BOL

Feeds 2
30 minutes

GRAB

- 2 handfuls minced meat (use Quorn or turkey mince for a leaner and often cheaper meal)
- Olive oil
- 2 large mushrooms, chopped (optional)
- 2 handfuls spaghetti or pasta – fusilli (the twisty one) is good
- Red Sauce (recipe on page 90)
- Salt and pepper

Try and stick to lean mince, as it contains less fat. To save money and add a higher nutritional value to your meal, substitute some of the meat with cooked mushrooms, courgettes, peppers or grated carrot. Also add aubergine or butter beans to add bulk and extra nutrients to help keep you energised for late-night cramming sessions.

GO

1 Put a large frying pan over a medium heat and add the mince with a *drizzle* of olive oil. Cook until *browned*, then add the chopped mushrooms, stir and cook for 10 minutes.

2 Bring a large pan of water to the boil. Add a pinch of salt and the spaghetti or pasta, with a teaspoon of olive oil to stop the pasta from sticking together. Leave to *simmer* on a low heat for 8 minutes or until *al dente*. Drain.

3 Drain the fat from the cooked meat, then stir in the red sauce. Season with salt and pepper to taste.

4 *Simmer* for 5 minutes over a low heat until hot, then serve with the spaghetti or pasta.

Goes well with:
Homemade Garlic Bread, page 106, All-in Salad, page 93, Roasted Veg Medley, page 112, Steamed Veg, page 119

EASY EATS

GOURMET TOAST

Feeds 1
10 minutes

GRAB

- 2 slices wholegrain or wholemeal bread
- Seasonings – salt and pepper, chilli flakes, mixed herbs
- Toppings of your choice. You could try: grated cheese and chopped cooked mushrooms; scrambled egg and crispy bacon; sliced cherry tomatoes, mixed herbs and torn mozzarella; or chopped cooked bacon and roast chicken.

GO

1 Place the bread on the grill and lightly toast it.

2 Place your chosen topping carefully onto the toast. Season as desired.

3 Pop under the grill for a couple of minutes and keep checking until the toppings are hot and any cheese you have used has melted. Tuck in!

Use wholegrain bread in this recipe to help keep you fuller for longer. Whole grains release energy slowly and can also reduce the risk of heart disease. This is a great snack because it can keep you going until your next meal and sets you up if you're planning to study in the evening.

LEMON, GARLIC AND HERB CHICKEN

Feeds 4
45 minutes

GRAB

- 2 tablespoons garlic puree
- 2 tablespoons lemon juice
- 2 tablespoons dried mixed herbs
- Pinch of salt
- 6 chicken pieces (thighs or legs), with skin

You can also use the lemon, garlic and herb mixture with chicken breast fillets, fish or even chicken wings.

Goes well with: Basmati Rice, page 98, Easy Cook Rice, page 98, Three Veg Mash, page CC, Cheesy Chive Potato Bake, page 42

This recipe is great because you get all the flavour without having to marinate the chicken for hours. The garlic adds to the tastiness and it also contains selenium, which is needed to keep the immune system in good working order. This recipe is delicious - great for date night!

EASY EATS

GO

1 Preheat the oven to 150°C/320°F/Gas Mark 2.

2 Warning: this can get a bit messy! In a bowl, mix together the garlic puree, lemon juice, salt and mixed herbs. Use your fingers to carefully pull back the skin from the chicken, then spread a thin layer of the mixture underneath the skin. Fold the skin back over the chicken.

3 Line a baking tray with kitchen foil, place the chicken on it and put in the oven for 30 minutes. *Baste* twice with the juices that run off the chicken. Check the inside of the chicken and make sure that no pink remains and the juices run clear. Leave to rest for a minute then serve.

RATATOUILLE

GRAB

Feeds 4
60 minutes

- 2 tablespoons olive oil
- 1 large aubergine, *cubed*
- 1 courgette, sliced into disks
- 1 red pepper, chopped
- 1 yellow pepper, chopped
- 1 red onion, chopped
- 2 cloves garlic, finely chopped
- Salt and pepper to taste
- 1 tin chopped tomatoes
- ½ glass red or white wine
- 1 squeeze tomato puree
- 1 teaspoon sugar
- Cooked rice or pasta to serve (optional)

Add a handful of cooked chickpeas to the mix to add more fibre – good for digestion!

GO

1 Put the oil into a large saucepan over a medium heat. Add the vegetables to the pan with salt and pepper to taste. Cover with a lid and *reduce* the heat. Allow to *simmer* and soften for 15 minutes. If you are using as a side dish, put on some rice or pasta so that it's ready when you've finished the ratatouille.

2 Now add the chopped tomatoes, red wine, squeeze of tomato puree and sugar. Stir thoroughly, then allow to *simmer* on a low heat for another 40 minutes with the lid off – this will help reduce the liquid. Stir occasionally.

3 Plate the ratatouille up by itself or with pasta or rice.

This recipe is great for getting a decent amount of veggies into your diet. It's also a nutritious yet hearty dish for vegetarians or vegans. Make it with your mates and share at the weekend.

SAM'S LAZY FISH PIE

GRAB

Feeds 4
40 minutes

- 200ml milk
- 5 cloves
- ½ an onion
- About 200g fish, chunked – you can use any white fish; haddock, cod, etc.
- 1 handful frozen peas
- 3 potatoes, peeled and cubed
- 200ml double cream
- 1 handful cooked prawns
- 5 teaspoons butter
- Salt and pepper to taste

You can serve this pie with broccoli and sweetcorn.

This is a very indulgent and tasty fish pie full of Omega 3 and protein. To make a version that's lower in fat, use skimmed milk and light butter and omit the cream, adding a teaspoon of cornflour instead.

EASY EATS

GO

1 Pour the milk into a medium pan on a medium heat. Push the cloves into the onion half and place into the milk. Add the fish and peas and bring to the boil.

2 Boil or *steam* the potatoes until soft, then mash with the butter and a teaspoon of milk.

3 After 10 minutes, or when the fish is cooked, remove the fish and peas and place them in an ovenproof dish along with the prawns. Remove the onion and discard.

4 Add the cream to the milk left in the pan and *simmer* until it *reduces* in volume by half.

5 Pour the milk/cream mixture over the fish mixture. Put the mash on top of the mixture and grill on a medium heat for 10–15 minutes or until the topping is golden brown.

SPICY STUFFED PEPPERS

Feeds 1-2
30 minutes

The different colours of peppers suggest the stage of maturity they are at, green being the earliest and then progressing to red. Peppers contain vitamins A, C and K, with red peppers having the highest intensity. This is a very tasty dish that looks impressive but is so simple to make - show off to your parents or use as a starter for a date.

GRAB

- 1 pack of flavoured couscous
- 2 red peppers
- ½ tin chopped tomatoes
- ½ red onion, finely chopped
- ½ tin sweetcorn
- ½ teaspoon chilli flakes
- 1 tablespoon olive oil

You can also use easy cook rice if you don't have any cous cous. You can make up to 6 stuffed peppers at once - just multiply the ingredients so that you have enough. Save the leftover ingredients for salads and snacks the next day.

GO

1 Preheat the oven to 200°C/400°F/Gas Mark 6.

2 Empty the couscous sachet into a bowl and add the required amount of water (refer to the packet). Leave to soak.

3 Cut the top off the peppers, making the 'hat' about the thickness of your thumb. Carefully scoop out the seeds from the inside so you just have empty shells.

4 Add the tomatoes, finely chopped red onion, sweetcorn and chilli flakes to the bowl of couscous and mix.

5 Fill the peppers with the mixture and place the hats back on them (they don't have to 'close'). *Drizzle* with olive oil and bake in an ovenproof dish in the pre-heated oven for 20 minutes.

 Goes well with: All-in Salad, page 93

SPICY VEG NOODLES

Feeds 1
15 minutes

GRAB

- 1 pepper, finely chopped
- 1 red onion, peeled and finely chopped
- 500 ml boiling water
- 1 chicken stock cube
- 1 packet chicken-flavoured noodles
- 1 teaspoon chilli powder
- 3 tablespoons tinned sweetcorn

You can omit the onion and pepper and instead add 1 scrambled egg and chopped ham to the noodles once they are cooked for a more savoury flavour.

GO

1 Fry the chopped pepper and onion in a teaspoon of olive oil until soft.

2 Pour in the boiling water and stir in the chicken stock cube until dissolved, along with the noodle flavour sachet and chilli powder. Stir well and bring back to the boil on a high heat.

3 Add the sweetcorn and noodles. Turn down to a *simmer* for 2 minutes, then stir thoroughly. *Simmer* with the lid off for another minute to *reduce* the liquid. Dig in!

EASY EATS

A very quick recipe that gives you a decent amount of carbs to keep you going. Adding vegetables to your noodles gives the meal more nutrients and takes it up that extra notch from a pot noodle.

STUFFED PITTAS

Feeds 1 pitta per person
10 minutes

GRAB

- 1 pack wholemeal pittas
- Butter (optional)
- Filling of your choice. Try any of these:
- Leftover sliced cooked chicken breast, chopped red onion, mayonnaise and tinned sweetcorn
- Torn cooked bacon, lettuce, sliced tomato and mayonnaise
- Cooked sliced sausage, salsa and lettuce
- Grated cheese, chopped red onion and pickle
- Leftover cooked chicken, cooked couscous, sliced tomato and cucumber
- Cooked couscous, chopped red pepper, chopped red onion
- Sliced cooked sausage, cheese and pickle
- Grated cheddar and sliced salami
- Falafel, lettuce, tomato and homemade Hummus (see recipe on page 89)
- All-in Salad (see recipe on page 93)
- Mozzarella slices, sliced tomato and Parma ham

I love making these - they're so easy and quick. Sandwiches are great for lunch at uni, but in a pitta the fillings can't fall out and you can pack more goodness in. Just the vitamin and mineral boost you need to help you stay energised through afternoon lectures. These pittas are a good way to use up leftovers too!

GO

I Place a pitta bread flat on a chopping board. Using a sharp knife, carefully make a curved cut from left to right just above the join of the bread – almost like a smile on top of the pitta. You can butter the inside of the pitta if you like.

2 Stuff with the filling of your choice and wrap in clingfilm to eat during the day when you are hungry.

SWEET AND SOUR CHICKEN

Feeds 2
35 minutes

GRAB

- 1 tablespoon olive oil
- 1 onion, chopped
- 1 small red chilli, deseeded and finely chopped
- 1 clove garlic, finely chopped
- 1 large chicken breast, *cubed*
- 1 teaspoon soy sauce
- 1 tablespoon tomato ketchup
- 1 teaspoon white vinegar
- 1 tablespoon honey
- 1 small tin pineapple chunks in juice

GO

1 Heat the oil in a medium saucepan. Add the chopped onion, chilli, garlic and chicken to the pan and fry until soft.

2 Now add the soy sauce, ketchup, vinegar, honey and the pineapple chunks with their juice. *Simmer* until the chicken is cooked through and the sauce thickens. If you prefer your sauce sweeter, just stir in a little more honey at the last minute.

It is healthier to make your own sweet and sour chicken than buy it from a takeaway, as many takeaway restaurants use a thick batter and sauces that contain the additive monosodium glutamate (MSG). If you're watching your weight, then making takeaway-style food yourself can help, as you can use different ingredients that are lower in fat but don't compromise on flavour. Adding pineapple and chillis helps to provide more nutritional value to your meal.

EASY EATS

Goes well with: Egg-Fried Rice,
page 104, Easy Cook Rice, page 98

SWEET CHILLI AND LIME PRAWN SKEWERS

Prawns are low in fat and very tasty, especially when combined with citrus flavours. Adding chilli not only gives more flavour to a dish, it has been suggested that an ingredient in the chilli helps to burn fat. I also find that adding chilli to my food helps when I have a cold. This recipe is great for a get-together and simple and quick to make!

Feeds 4
40 minutes (+ marinating time)

GRAB

* 1 small pack of king prawns
* 1 tablespoon garlic puree
* A pinch of black pepper
* Juice of ½ a lime (you can also use ½ a lemon)
* Another lime or lemon for squeezing over the skewers
* 1 red chilli, deseeded and chopped
* Wooden or metal skewers

GO

1 Place the prawns in a medium-sized non-metallic bowl. Add the garlic puree, pepper, lime or lemon juice and chopped chilli. Stir all the ingredients together. Cover the bowl with clingfilm and leave for at least 30 minutes to *marinate* – you don't have to, but the marinade really flavours the prawns.

2 If you're using wooden skewers, soak them beforehand in water for at least 25 minutes to make them more resistant to flames.

3 Remove the prawns from the marinade. Thread the prawns onto the skewers one at a time lengthways, so when the skewer is laid flat you can see the whole prawn. Leave at least a thumb's length at the end of each skewer.

4 Grill for 3 minutes on each side under a medium grill and serve with lime or lemon quarters.

Goes well with: Basmati Rice, page 98, Homemade Garlic Bread, page 106, Speedy Couscous Salad, page 116, Sour Cream and Chive dip, page 87

EASY EATS

TOMATO SPINACH PENNE

Spinach is high in vitamins, including vitamin K, which helps to promote a healthy nervous system and supports your brain function. You can boil or steam spinach lightly and add it to pretty much anything. This is a really simple meal that can also be eaten cold – great for lunch!

Feeds 1
10 minutes

GRAB

- 1 teaspoon olive oil
- 1 handful penne
- 1 handful spinach
- 1 tin chopped tomatoes

I like to use penne pasta because the tube shape traps the sauce inside it making it extra juicy, but you can use any shaped pasta or even spaghetti.

GO

1 Bring a pan of water to the boil, add a teaspoon of olive oil and cook the pasta gently until firm. Just as the pasta starts to become soft, add the spinach so it can cook alongside the pasta. You can alternatively boil the pasta in the bottom tier of a steamer and then steam the spinach for a minute in the top tier if preferred.

2 When both are cooked, drain and return to the pan. Pour in the tinned tomatoes. *Simmer* gently for 2–3 minutes or until the mixture is piping hot, then serve immediately.

Goes well with: Homemade Garlic Bread, page 106

TUNA PASTA BAKE

GRAB

Feeds 2
30 minutes

- Olive oil
- Salt
- 2 handfuls pasta twists
- 1 small red onion, finely chopped
- 1 can tuna fish, drained
- 1 tablespoon cornflour
- 200ml milk
- Handful grated cheese plus extra for topping
- ½ can sweetcorn

If you aren't partial to onion, try a handful of chopped chives instead for a more subtle flavour.

GO

1 Preheat the oven to 200°C/400°F/Gas Mark 6.

2 Bring a medium saucepan of water to the boil and stir in a pinch of salt and a teaspoon of olive oil. Add the pasta and boil until it's *al dente*, then drain the water from the pan. In a small saucepan, fry the chopped onion in a splash of olive oil until soft, then add to the pasta along with the drained tuna and sweetcorn.

3 Put the cornflour in a small saucepan and gradually add the milk. Keep stirring all the time so that the mixture doesn't become lumpy, and bring to the boil. Remove from the heat and add the handful of grated cheese to the mixture.

4 Pour the cheese sauce over the tuna and pasta mixture and stir until all the ingredients are combined. Use a spatula to scoop the mix into an ovenproof dish, then top with more grated cheese.

5 Bake in the oven until the cheese is golden brown on top.

EASY EATS

Omega 3 fatty acids, found in tuna, are essential for a healthy metabolism. This bake is great for sharing with friends!

TURKEY RISOTTO

Feeds 1
20 minutes

Turkey is one of the cheapest meats, yet it is still rich in protein and very lean. You can use turkey fillets or turkey mince in this recipe. It cooks quickly and absorbs flavour well, so it would be a good meal to munch on while revising. This isn't a classic risotto, but it's easy and tasty!

GRAB

- 1 red onion, peeled and finely chopped
- ½ red pepper, finely chopped
- ½ yellow pepper, finely chopped
- 1 turkey fillet, *cubed*
- Teaspoon butter
- ½ tsp chilli flakes
- 2 chicken stock cubes
- 1½ mugs boiling water
- ⅓ mug long-grain rice
- ½ tin of sweetcorn

Serve with crusty bread.

GO

1 Fry the chopped onion, peppers and turkey in a saucepan with the butter until soft, then add the chilli flakes. Dissolve the stock cubes in the boiling water according to the instructions on the packaging and add to the saucepan.

2 Bring back to the boil, add the rice and *simmer* over a medium heat until all the water is *reduced* (pretty much soaked up!) and the turkey is cooked through. Stir occasionally to make sure the liquid is distributed.

3 Add the sweetcorn and heat gently until hot.

YOU CHOOSE STIR-FRY

Feeds 2
20 minutes

Stir-fries are cheap, easy to make and you can add pretty much whatever leftovers you have in the fridge or store cupboard. This dish is great for getting in several of your five a day. You choose the ingredients in stir-fries and there's lots of room to experiment. Also, you don't have to use egg noodles - why not try rice noodles, or brown or white rice?

GRAB

- 1 tablespoon olive oil
- 2 handfuls meat or seafood of your choice – sliced pork, *diced* chicken, strips of beef, king prawns...
- 2 cloves garlic, finely chopped
- 2 spring onions, sliced
- 1 red pepper, sliced
- 1 pack stir-fry veg or grated carrot, beansprouts, sliced mushrooms and chopped cabbage
- 1 pack egg noodles
- 1 tablespoon soy sauce
- Sweet chilli sauce or another sauce of your choice

GO

1 Add the oil to a wok. When the oil is hot, toss in the meat and cook for 5 minutes (or until the meat is no longer pink in the middle). Now add the finely chopped garlic, spring onions and red peppers. Stir-fry for another 5 minutes.

2 Add the rest of the stir-fry veg, noodles and soy sauce, and stir-fry for another 5 minutes.

3 Add the sauce of your choice and *simmer* for 1 minute, then serve.

SOUPS AND STEWS

CARIBBEAN CHICKEN SOUP

GRAB

Feeds 6
60 minutes

- 1 large white potato, peeled and chopped
- 1 sweet potato, peeled and chopped
- 2 carrots, peeled and chopped
- 2 onions, peeled and chopped
- 3 spring onions, roots and outer leaves discarded and stalks chopped
- 3 cloves of garlic, *crushed*
- 1 packet chicken/chicken noodle soup mix
- 1 chicken stock cube
- ½ a roast chicken or cooked chicken breast fillet
- 1 teaspoon mixed herbs
- Salt and pepper to taste

GO

1 Put 2 pints of water into a large pan. Put the lid on the pan and set over a high heat.

2 Add all the vegetables to the water. When the water is at boiling point, add the soup mix and stir in.

3 Put a small amount of the boiling water into a mug and dissolve the stock cube in it, then pour back into the pan. Tear the meat off the

> This soup is low in fat and also gives you a balanced meal of protein and vegetables. For me, this was a reading week winner: make, freeze, and eat when you need. Not only does this keep your energy topped up, it helps you avoid wasting money on takeaways when you need maximum study time.

½ chicken and add, leaving some meat on the bones for flavour.

4 Boil the soup until the potatoes are soft and break up when you pierce them with a fork. Then turn the heat down and *simmer* for another 15 minutes.

5 Remove the chicken bones and serve the soup immediately with crusty bread. You could also divide it into smaller containers, cool and freeze, or keep in the fridge for a couple of days and eat during the week.

Goes well with: Homemade Garlic Bread, page 106

SOUPS AND STEWS

CARROT AND CORIANDER SOUP

Feeds 6-8
60 minutes

Carrots contain more vitamin A than any other vegetable. Vitamin A can boost energy production - perfect for a day of lectures and an essay deadline the next day. Soups are great student meals - you can freeze them and have a hearty, healthy meal ready in minutes.

GRAB

- 1 tablespoon olive oil
- 1 large onion, peeled and chopped
- 6 carrots, peeled and *cubed*
- 2 potatoes, peeled and *cubed*
- 2 cloves garlic, chopped
- Half a pint of stock – I dissolve 2 vegetable stock cubes in half a pint of boiling water
- 1 handful fresh coriander, leaves stripped from stalks and chopped
- Salt and pepper
- Helen's Hot Pepper Sauce (see recipe on page 88; optional)

You can add another potato to make the soup thicker or add a tablespoon of crème fraîche for a creamier taste.

GO

1 Heat the oil in the pan on a medium heat. Add the chopped onion and fry until soft. Add the *cubed* carrots, potatoes, chopped garlic and stock. Turn up the heat and boil on a high heat for 20 minutes. Pop the lid on and *simmer* for another 20 minutes, or until you can pierce through the veggies with a knife.

2 Leave to cool for 2 minutes. Put the contents of the pan into a blender with the chopped coriander. Blend until smooth then add salt and pepper to taste. Hot pepper sauce adds a bit of a kick – just a dash will do.

 Goes well with: Homemade Garlic Bread, page 106

CHUNKY VEG SOUP

Feeds 4
50 minutes

GRAB

- 1 teaspoon butter
- 1 clove of garlic, *crushed*
- 1 small white/red onion, peeled and chopped
- 2 carrots, peeled and chopped
- 6 broccoli *florets*
- ½ can sweetcorn (use the rest in Tuna and Sweetcorn Chilli Pasta, see recipe on page 124)
- 1 large white potato, peeled and chopped
- Boiling water
- 1 vegetable stock cube
- 1 tablespoon cornflour
- ½ teaspoon chilli flakes
- Salt and pepper

Soup is a great student brain food because it can help keep you hydrated when you're studying for long periods and it includes nutritious veggies. It also stores well and you only have one bowl and spoon to wash up – leaving more time for study and socialising.

GO

1 Heat the butter in a large pan, and add the crushed garlic. Next, add the onion, carrots, broccoli *florets*, sweetcorn and potato.

2 Pour 1 litre of boiling water into the pan with the vegetables.

3 Boil over a medium heat for 10 minutes, then crumble the stock cube into the soup. Add 1 tablespoon cornflour mixed with 1 tablespoon cold water, then *simmer* for another 15 minutes or until the potatoes are soft and break up when you pierce them with a fork. Add the chilli flakes and season to taste with salt and pepper.

CLAIRE'S LENTIL STEW

GRAB

Feeds 4
40 minutes

- 1 baking potato, peeled and *cubed*
- 1 clove garlic, peeled and *crushed*
- 1 onion, peeled and chopped
- 1 teaspoon olive oil
- 1 leek, trimmed and chopped
- ½ red pepper, chopped
- 2 large carrots, peeled and chopped
- Boiling water
- 2 vegetable stock cubes
- 2 teaspoons bouillon powder
- 1 mug red lentils

Serve with French stick or crusty rolls.

GO

1 Boil or steam the potatoes for 10 minutes. Drain and place in a large pan.

2 Fry the garlic and onion in oil until soft and add to the potatoes in the large pan. Add the leek, pepper and carrots to the large pan.

3 Pour over enough boiling water to cover the vegetables, then add the stock cubes, bouillon powder and lentils, and stir. Cover and leave to cook over a low heat until the lentils are soft. Check after 20 minutes. If the lentils are still hard, add half a mug of boiling water and cook for a further few minutes. Serve immediately.

I met Claire on the train when I was writing this book - she was a student and cheerfully shared her healthy lentil stew recipe with me. Lentils are often overlooked, but they actually make a very filling meal. They also contain a high amount of fibre, making them a cheap alternative to meat.

CLASSIC TOMATO SOUP

Feeds 4
60 minutes

GRAB

- 10 medium-large tomatoes (or 2 cans of tinned tomatoes)
- 2 cloves garlic, peeled and chopped
- 1 large onion, peeled and chopped
- 1 large carrot, peeled and chopped
- 1 teaspoon olive oil
- 2 chicken/vegetable stock cubes
- 1 tablespoon ketchup
- 1 tablespoon tomato puree
- Salt and black pepper to taste

Tomato soup is not only warm, filling and a great comfort food - it helps to aid weight loss if you're dieting, as it's low in calories. Tomatoes contain at least five different vitamins and can lower the risk of heart disease, so making a load of them into soup could be very beneficial if you're looking for a quick, healthy snack, perhaps after the gym or work.

For a more tangy flavour blend in a red pepper, deseeded and chopped.

GO

1 Prepare the tomatoes by pulling out the green tops. Quarter them and scoop out the lighter part of the tomato, which has all the seeds in it.

2 Put the garlic, onion and carrot into a large pan over a medium heat with a teaspoon olive oil. Fry until soft, stirring occasionally so that the mixture doesn't burn or stick to the pan. *Simmer* over a medium heat for about 5 minutes, then stir again and leave for another 5 minutes.

3 Dilute the stock cubes according to the instructions on the packaging, then add the stock to the veg mixture. Stir thoroughly.

4 Now add the tomatoes or tinned tomatoes, ketchup and tomato puree, stirring well. Put the lid on the pan and cook for 30 minutes. Check at least twice and give the soup a stir to make sure the ingredients are distributed equally.

5 Now taste the soup and add more seasoning if you like. Cool for 5 minutes, then pour into a blender. Do not overfill – blend a bit at a time, making sure there is a large gap at the top.

6 Eat immediately or cool and then freeze for up to 2 months in small batches.

SOUPS AND STEWS

GARLIC AND BUTTERNUT SQUASH SOUP

Feeds 4
45 minutes

GRAB

- 1 tablespoon olive oil
- 4 cloves garlic, peeled and finely chopped
- 1 onion, peeled and finely chopped
- 1 large butternut squash, peeled
- 1 carrot, peeled and cubed
- 1 large baking potato or two medium potatoes, peeled and *cubed*
- 1 vegetable stock cube
- Boiling water
- Salt and pepper to season
- 1 teaspoon garlic salt (optional – I love the taste of garlic!)

Serve with crusty bread and butter.

GO

1 Put the oil in a large pan and place over a medium heat. Add the garlic and onion to the pan and leave to cook down until soft.

2 Halve the butternut squash lengthways. Scoop out the seeds in the middle and *cube* the flesh. Add to the pan with the carrot and potato and cook for about 20 minutes.

3 Put the stock cube into a mug and fill to halfway with boiling water. Mash it down with a tablespoon and stir until dissolved. Add to the pan with 2 pints of boiling water from the kettle. *Simmer* until the vegetables are soft.

4 Allow the soup to cool for 5 minutes, then blend until smooth. Add salt and pepper as needed plus garlic salt if you like.

Garlic can help keep
your blood pressure down and
butternut squash is low in calories. When you've got
a deadline to keep and you've had a long day, it's lovely to
come home, pop your pre-made soup in a pan for a
few minutes and tuck in.

HEARTY BEEF STEW

Feeds 4
2 ½ hours

This is good in the winter when it's chilly or when you just fancy a hearty, no-fuss meal. It also freezes well. You get your protein, carbs and vegetables in one hit and fuel up on slow-release energy. Great for a last-minute cramming session!

GRAB

- Boiling water
- 1 large onion, peeled and chopped
- 2 spring onions, trimmed and chopped
- 1 teaspoon olive oil
- 440g or two big handfuls of *diced* beef
- Plain flour
- 2 large carrots, peeled and chopped
- 1 potato, peeled and chopped
- 2 beef/chicken stock cubes
- Pinch of pepper
- 1 teaspoon garlic salt (optional)
- 2 sprigs thyme (optional)

Serve with crusty granary or wholegrain bread or over rice.

You can add 1 chopped tomato and a teaspoon of Helen's Hot Pepper Sauce (see recipe on page 88) to give the stew a tangy flavour.

GO

1 Fill a very large pot with 2.5 pints of boiling water from the kettle; keep it over a high heat so that it stays hot.

2 Fry the chopped onion and spring onion in the olive oil in a separate pan until soft.

3 Put the meat in a bowl and cover with plain flour – mix with your hands so that the meat is lightly covered, then add to the onions and fry for 3 minutes. Stir to *brown* the meat on all sides.

4 Add the chopped carrots and potato to the pan of boiling water.

5 Put the stock cubes in a mug and use a ladle to add boiling water from the pan until the mug is half full. Stir until the stock cubes are dissolved and pour back into the pan. Now add the meat and onions to the pan and stir twice.

6 Turn down the heat and let the stew *simmer* for at least 2 hours or until the beef is tender. Add the garlic salt, pepper and thyme to season.

SOUPS AND STEWS

DIPS AND SAUCES

GUACAMOLE

GRAB

- 1 ripe avocado
- Salt and pepper to season
- ½ teaspoon chilli flakes
- Juice of 1 lime
- 2 garlic cloves, *crushed*

Serve with tortilla chips, crisps, crusty bread or even spread it on toast.

Feeds 1-2
10 minutes

GO

1 Using a sharp knife, slice the avocado in half, moving the knife around the stone. Twist the two halves apart, peel off the skin and discard the stone.

2 Place the avocado flesh in a bowl. Add the seasoning, lime juice and garlic. Mash with a fork until smooth.

3 Spoon into a small ramekin or pot.

As well as being creamy and tasty, an avocado contains more than 20 vitamins and minerals - a great energy boost during study days. You can also use guacamole as a filling in a roll - see the deep-fill sandwich recipes on page 48 for more ideas.

See overleaf for image of the prepared dip

SALSA

Feeds 4
10 minutes

GRAB

- 1 tablespoon olive oil
- 1 red onion, finely chopped
- 2 green chillies, deseeded and finely chopped
- ½ green pepper, finely chopped
- 3 large tomatoes, chopped
- 1 small handful fresh coriander (about 6 stalks), finely chopped
- ¼ teaspoon sugar
- Salt and pepper to taste

Add tinned sweetcorn to the salsa to make it extra juicy. Eat with tortillas, pittas or even on a hotdog!

Goes well with: Easy Sharing Wraps, page 138

GO

1   Heat olive oil in a pan over a low heat. Add the finely chopped onions, chillies and peppers and cook until softened.

2 Add the chopped tomatoes, stir and *simmer* for 10 minutes.

3 Add the finely chopped coriander and sugar, and season to taste with salt and pepper.

Shop-bought salsa can be very high in sodium (salt), so it's best to make it at home. You can use homemade fresh salsa as an alternative to ketchup, which contains a lot of sugar and doesn't compare when it comes to nutritional value!

SOUR CREAM AND CHIVE

Feeds 2
5 minutes

DIPS AND SAUCES

GRAB

- 150ml reduced-fat sour cream
- 7 fresh chives, finely chopped
- Juice of ½ lemon
- Salt and pepper

Serve with Best BBQ Wings (page 34) or tortilla chips for movie night.

GO

1 Pour the sour cream into a bowl and stir in the lemon juice.

2 Stir the chives into the cream. Taste and add salt and pepper to season. Spoon into a small bowl and set on a plate surrounded with tortilla chips or nachos.

Chives are part of the onion family and contain beta carotene, which helps to maintain the immune system. You can also add this sauce to cooked new potatoes to make a speedy potato salad.

HELEN'S HOT PEPPER SAUCE

GRAB

20+
10 minutes

- 2 Scotch bonnet peppers, finely chopped (with stalks removed)
- 6½ tablespoons malt vinegar
- 6½ tablespoons olive oil
- 2 cloves garlic, finely chopped
- ½ teaspoon salt

If you want a milder hot pepper sauce, use a whole red bell pepper or a large deseeded red chilli instead of Scotch bonnet peppers.

GO

1 Wear tightly fitting rubber or latex gloves when chopping the peppers to avoid trapping any of the flesh under your nails, as it is very hot. Also, do not put your fingers in your mouth or eyes (or anyone else's!) after handling the peppers, as the pepper juices can burn.

2 Put the peppers and garlic in a blender, add the rest of the ingredients and blend until smooth.

3 Pour into a glass jar with a tightly fitting lid and leave in a cupboard for 4 days.

4 Use just ½ a teaspoon in your meals for a zingy, hot flavour.

Scotch bonnet peppers are quite hot, so you only need a tiny bit of this sauce - a few drops is enough. I add this sauce to my chilli con carne (see page 144) to help get rid of a blocked nose!

Goes well with: Larry's Chilli Con Carne, page 144, Easy Spag Bol, page 50, Caribbean Chicken Soup, page 73 – or anything else you want to add some spice to!

HUMMUS

DIPS AND SAUCES

> Chickpeas contain a lot of fibre, which helps you feel fuller for longer. If you're trying to lose weight, substitute a pile of cheesy nachos with raw vegetable sticks and homemade hummus - they're just as tasty! Hummus is also great to eat with a warm pitta as a snack when revising.

Feeds 2
10 minutes

GRAB

- 1 can of chickpeas, drained
- Juice of 1 lemon
- 3 tablespoons olive oil
- 3 garlic cloves, *crushed*
- ½ teaspoon chilli powder
- Salt and pepper
- 1 tablespoon water

Hummus is a Turkish dish, so if you want a more authentic taste to your hummus add 1 tablespoon tahini - you should be able to find it in most supermarkets. Tahini is a paste made from ground white sesame seeds and peanut oil and adds a very nutty flavour.

Serve with raw vegetable sticks like peeled carrots and cucumber, cooked potato wedges or warm pitta bread.

GO

1 Place the drained chickpeas in a medium bowl or container.

2 Add 1 tablespoon water, garlic, chilli powder and lemon juice. Mash down with a fork, adding the olive oil gradually as you do. If you can, blend the mixture to make it even smoother.

RED SAUCE

GRAB

Feeds 2
30 minutes

- 1 small onion, chopped
- 2 garlic cloves, *crushed*
- 1 tablespoon olive oil
- 2 cans chopped tomatoes
- 2 teaspoons dried mixed herbs
- Salt and pepper to taste
- 1 tablespoon tomato ketchup (optional)

GO

1 Cook the onion and garlic in the olive oil in a pan over a low heat until soft. Add the tomatoes, mixed herbs and salt and pepper.

2 *Simmer* with the lid on for about 20 minutes, until the ingredients have become soft. Stir in the ketchup and add salt and pepper to taste – you're done! If you want a really smooth sauce you can blend for 20 seconds.

Goes well with: Lasagne, page 146, Easy Spag Bol, page 50

> Making your own sauces means that you can add more vegetables and therefore more vitamins and minerals. If you make it at home you can bet it will have fewer additives and colourings than a shop-bought sauce, too, as well as being cheaper. You can freeze this sauce for up to three months, then simply defrost in the fridge when you want to use it.

WHITE SAUCE

Feeds 2
10 minutes

GRAB

- 2 tablespoons butter
- 3 tablespoons flour
- Mug of cold milk

GO

I You can't leave the stove when making this sauce otherwise it could go lumpy and burn. In a non-stick pan, melt the butter over a medium heat until it is completely liquid.

2 Add the flour bit by bit, stirring as you go. The flour will start to absorb the butter. What you are aiming for is a roux or stiff paste. After all the flour is combined, slowly pour in half the milk, stirring continuously.

3 Stir in the rest of the milk slowly. Use elbow grease to stir until the sauce is smooth with no lumps.

White sauce is very, very cheap to make. If you need a sauce for pasta, chicken or even potatoes, this could be the one for you - it's so versatile. The ingredients are simple and natural, unlike the variety in a jar, which contains preservatives and additives. When you're down to your last fiver, choose homemade versions of what you like and save your money!

DIPS AND SAUCES

SIMPLE SIDES

ALL-IN SALAD

Feeds 1
10 minutes

GRAB

- 1 carrot, grated
- Handful cherry tomatoes
- Lettuce, shredded
- Red cabbage, grated
- Cucumber, sliced
- Radishes, sliced
- Celery, sliced
- Green or red pepper, sliced
- Creamed horseradish to taste (optional)

Try mixing in tuna and chopped onion to make a healthy packed lunch.

Mixed salads are a great way to get portions of your five a day. If you're trying to detox from pot noodles and kebabs, then a fresh all-in salad is a great starting point. You can just use what's in the fridge, but the more veg you can mix in the better! Salad can be made in advance and grabbed when you need it, saving you time when you're studying.

GO

1 Choose your veggies. Put into a large bowl and toss to mix everything up.

2 An optional squeeze of lemon juice and black pepper, or dried mixed herbs and a teaspoon of mayonnaise, makes a thrifty alternative to salad dressing.

AVOCADO, CHICKEN & BACON SALAD

Feeds 1
10 minutes

GRAB

- Lettuce (little gem lettuce is best for this salad as it has small leaves), washed and torn
- 2 rashers bacon
- 4 cherry tomatoes, quartered
- 1 ripe avocado
- ¼ roast chicken
- Black pepper
- 1 teaspoon olive oil

Replace the chicken and bacon with cooked king prawns and a squirt of lemon juice for a lighter version.

GO

1 Chop the bacon into strips and grill under a medium heat or fry in a splash of olive oil until crispy. (Remember to use separate chopping boards for meat and veg.)

2 Place the avocado lengthways on a chopping board. Use a knife to slice down to the stone and follow the first slice all the way around until you have two halves. Twist to separate. Discard the stone, scoop out the flesh with a teaspoon and *cube* it.

3 Tear the chicken into small strips and mix it with all the other ingredients in a bowl. Season with black pepper and *drizzle* over some olive oil.

DR OPARA'S FOOD FOR THOUGHT
A junk food lunch will fill you up, but how long until you begin to feel peckish and all you can think about is food and not the book chapter or journal article you have to read to get your head round that assignment?

Avocados can provide more than 25 essential nutrients, including the anti-oxident vitamins A, C and E. Eat one mashed with black pepper and spread on wholemeal toast before an exam for slow-release energy.

Goes well with: Lasagne, page 146

BAKED MACARONI CHEESE

Feeds 4
30 minutes

GRAB

- 4 handfuls macaroni
- White Sauce (see recipe on page 91)
- Salt and black pepper
- 1 handful grated Cheddar cheese
- Tablespoon dried mixed herbs

Cheese contains calcium, which is essential for the growth and development of your bones, so it can be good for you in small amounts. If you're trying to cut down on carbs, why not try adding chopped mushrooms and ham as a substitute for some of the pasta?

GO

| Put the macaroni in a large pan of boiling water and leave to cook for around 8 minutes until *al dente*. Drain and set aside.

2 Make the white sauce.

3 Preheat the oven to 160°C/325°F/Gas Mark 3.

4 Add the cooked macaroni to the white sauce, sprinkle in some salt and pepper to season and stir. Pour the mixture into an ovenproof dish, sprinkle the cheese on top with some dried mixed herbs.

5 Bake in the oven 10 minutes or until the cheese is golden brown on top.

Goes well with: All-in Salad, page 93, Best BBQ Wings, page 34, Roast Chicken, page 156

BASMATI RICE (+ EASY COOK RICE)

Feeds 2
30 minutes

GRAB

- White or brown basmati rice
- Olive oil
- Salt

Basmati rice has a nuttier flavour than easy cook or long grain. You can also get brown basmati rice, which is more nutritious because the outside of the wheat is left on. Why not try it or mix it with the white basmati rice?

GO

1 For two people use 1 small cup of rice. Put it in a sieve and rinse until the water runs clear – this stops the rice from sticking together.

2 Put the rice in a medium pan over a low heat with a few drops of olive oil and a pinch of salt, and 2 small cup fulls of cold water. Bring it to the boil, then cover with a lid on and leave for 20 minutes. When the grains are dry the rice is cooked – do not stir it while cooking.

3 Fluff the rice up with a fork and serve.

Easy cook rice is made the same way except you don't have to rinse the rice.
Alternatively, just ask for a rice cooker before you go to uni or pick one up cheaply at your local supermarket - it's so much easier!

You can add mixed herbs and a handful of wild rice to make your dish look more impressive.

SIMPLE SIDES

I live in a Caribbean household, which means that rice is in a lot of our recipes. After too many burned pans to mention, I finally got it right! This rice takes longer to make than you might expect, so I suggest putting it on before you start prepping the rest of your meal.

BLACK PEPPER MASH

Feeds 2
20 minutes

Black pepper is said to help with digestion. Added to the mash, this makes s simple side that complements almost any main in this book, but also helps your stomach to break all the food down. If you're feeling stressed out by your schedule, add some black pepper to your food to combat indigestion.

SIMPLE SIDES

GRAB

- 2 large potatoes, peeled
- Milk
- 1 teaspoon butter
- 1 teaspoon ground black peppercorns or black pepper
- Salt

For a different flavour mash, season with chilli flakes instead of black pepper.

GO

1 *Steam* or boil the potatoes until they break up easily when pierced with a fork.

2 Use a potato masher to *crush* the potatoes until they are light and fluffy. Add a tablespoon of milk if they are looking too dry.

3 Add the butter and then the pepper. Add salt to season, stir and serve while hot.

Goes well with: Mango Lamb Chops, page 149, Lemon, Garlic and Herb Chicken, page 53

CAESAR SALAD

The dressing makes up the majority of the fat content in this recipe, so opt for a low-fat Caesar dressing if you can. This salad is a great way to use up leftover chicken.

Feeds 1
10 minutes

GRAB

- Cooked chicken breast
- Little gem lettuce
- Handful of grated Cheddar cheese (or low-fat torn mozzarella for a lower-fat option)
- Slice of brown bread or a handful of ready-made croutons
- Olive oil
- Caesar salad dressing

Squeeze of lemon juice for extra tang

GO

1 Tear the chicken breast into chunks or strips and place in a large bowl. Tear up 2 leaves of the lettuce and add to the bowl with a handful of grated cheese.

2 Use ready-made croutons or make your own by cutting the bread into cubes and frying in a teaspoon of olive oil until toasted brown on all sides.

3 Leave the croutons to cool and mix in with the other ingredients. *Drizzle* on some Caesar salad dressing and lemon juice and tuck in!

DIY COLESLAW

Feeds 2
10 minutes

GRAB

- 4 carrots, peeled and grated
- ½ onion, peeled and grated
- ½ white cabbage, grated
- 3 tablespoons low-fat mayonnaise
- 2 tablespoons natural yoghurt
- 1 teaspoon honey
- black pepper
- 1 teaspoon Dijon mustard

You can also use red cabbage and beansprouts to make an even crunchier coleslaw, or for a sweeter taste add raisins or dried apricots, which are a good source of magnesium and potassium.

Shop-bought coleslaw often uses high-fat mayonnaise. It's cheaper to make it yourself and you can use natural yoghurt instead and lessen the fat content. Cabbage can boost your immunuity and carrots contain beta carotene, which helps to maintain your cells. Coleslaw makes a great side if you're skint!

GO

1 Put the grated carrots, onion and cabbage into a bowl.
2 Combine the mayonnaise, yoghurt, honey, a twist of black pepper and mustard. Stir into the salad and eat.

Goes well with: Roast Chicken, page 156, Adam's Homemade Burgers, page 133, Baked Potato, page 31, Best BBQ Wings, page 34, Lemon, Garlic and Herb Chicken, page 53

EGG-FRIED RICE

Feeds 4
40 minutes

GRAB

- 2 spring onions
- 1 tablespoon olive oil
- 200g or 4 handfuls cooked and cooled basmati or long grain rice (cool quickly by putting in a bowl and standing that in cold water)
- 1 large egg, *beaten* (with a fork in a mug)
- 1 tablespoon soy sauce
- 1 teaspoon ground white pepper (you can use black pepper if you don't have white, but white pepper gives a more authentic taste)
- 3 tablespoons frozen peas, defrosted (or use fresh)

To make special fried rice just add some cooked prawns, ham and some leftover strips of roast chicken.

GO

1 Remove the root end from the spring onions and strip off the outer leaves. Chop up to the dark green part. Place the chopped onion to one side.

2 Heat a wok until medium hot, then add the oil. Swirl around the wok.

3 Add the chopped onion and peas, stir-frying for about 2–3 minutes until cooked through. Add the cold cooked rice and toss with a wooden spatula for a further 2–3 minutes, making sure you scrape the bottom of the wok.

4 Make a hole in the middle of the rice and pour the beaten egg into it bit by bit, keep stirring and adding until the egg is scrambling and is distributed throughout the rice.

5 Season with soya sauce and pepper. Remove from the heat and plate up.

Goes well with: Sweet and Sour Chicken, page 62, Best BBQ Wings, page 34

Takeaway egg-fried rice is often fried in a lot of unhealthy oil. Make it at home to control what's going into your food and keep an eye on the fat content. Use cold cooked rice in this recipe because then it won't stick together in the wok.

HOMEMADE GARLIC BREAD

Feeds 4
20 minutes

GRAB

- 1 granary or wholemeal French stick
- 1 clove garlic, very finely chopped
- 2 tablespoons butter

If you want to make milder garlic bread just spread a thin layer of garlic paste on top of each slice of French stick, instead of the garlic mixed with butter. You can also make cheesy garlic bread by following this recipe but topping each slice with a thin layer or grated mozzarella or Cheddar and grilling.

Why splash out on a supermarket garlic baguette that's loaded with salt and additives? Save your money and waistline by making your own. It's very simple and I think this version tastes even yummier! Fresh garlic can help to keep your blood pressure down, which is good for those days when you're feeling stressed out.

GO

I Slice the French stick into medium slices about an inch thick. Lay them out on an oven tray lined with kitchen foil.

2 Place the chopped garlic in a bowl. Add the butter and mix the two together – try to make sure the garlic is distributed evenly.

3 Spread a thin layer of the mixture on top of each slice of bread. Place the tray under a medium grill or in the oven at 150°C/300°F/Gas Mark 2 until golden brown. Serve while hot.

Goes well with: Puff Pastry Pizza, page 154, Mini Movie Pizzas, page 152, Best BBQ Wings, page 34, All-in Salad, page 93, Lasagne, page 146

SIMPLE SIDES

ITALIAN SALAD

Feeds 2
10 minutes

GRAB

- 1 ball mozzarella cheese, *cubed*
- 8 cherry tomatoes, halved
- Handful fresh basil leaves
- Olive oil

Sliced black olives add a really zingy flavour to this salad.

GO

1 Put the cubed mozzarella in a bowl with the halved cherry tomatoes.

2 Rinse the basil leaves in cold water, then mix with the cheese and tomatoes.

3 Add a *drizzle* of olive oil and tuck in!

This salad has three main ingredients, is light, quick and tasty, and will feed 2 as a side dish or 1 as a snack! Tomatoes contain many vitamins which may help to boost your immune system, and mozzarella contains zinc, which is said to help prevent colds. This makes the recipe great for winter or after a bout of heavy studying.

Goes well with: Lasagne, page 146, Best BBQ Wings, page 34

NEW POTATOES

Most of the nutrients in potatoes are actually in and just below the skin, so leave it on! Potatoes are a cheap source of carbohydrates and, when eaten in moderation, can help balance your diet. If you don't have the time for roast potatoes, new potatoes are a quicker alternative and just as delicious!

GRAB

- 1 handful small new potatoes
- 1 tablespoon butter
- 1 teaspoon dried mixed herbs
- 1 teaspoon garlic salt
- 1 teaspoon black pepper

Feeds 1
15 minutes

GO

1 *Steam* or boil the potatoes until you can pierce them easily with a knife.

2 Drain and place in a medium bowl. Add the butter, herbs, salt and pepper and stir until blended. Serve while hot.

Goes well with: Baked Sweet Chilli Salmon, page 32, Roast Chicken, page 156

POTATO SALAD

Feeds 4
20 minutes

GRAB

- 3 medium potatoes, *cubed*
- 1 handful fresh chives, chopped
- 1 red onion, peeled and finely chopped
- 2 tablespoons low-fat mayonnaise
- 1 tablespoon mustard

GO

1 Boil or *steam* the potatoes until soft.

2 Put the chives and red onion in a medium bowl. Add the mayonnaise and mustard and stir.

3 Add the potatoes to the bowl and stir until well covered in dressing.

The mustard in this potato salad not only gives it a zingy flavour, it's also high in antioxidants – great for helping to repair damage after a night out. Also a very cheap side dish to take to parties or picnics!

Goes well with: Mango Lamb Chops, page 149, Adam's Homemade Burgers, page 133, Best BBQ Wings, page 34, Roast Chicken, page 156

ROASTED VEG MEDLEY

Feeds 4
40 minutes

GRAB

- 2 small red onions, peeled and quartered
- 2 carrots, peeled and *cubed*
- 2 parsnips, peeled and *cubed*
- ½ butternut squash, peeled and *cubed*
- 1 sweet potato, peeled and *cubed* (you can alternatively use a normal white potato)
- 1 clove garlic, finely chopped
- 4 tablespoons olive oil
- 3 sprigs thyme
- 2 sprigs rosemary
- 1 tablespoon clear honey

Orange vegetables are rich in vitamins, contain beta carotene and antioxidants and could help your eyes, skin and heart – sounds like a winner considering how much time we spend reading, writing, surfing the internet and typing as students!

GO

1 Preheat the oven to 200°C/400°F/Gas Mark 6.

2 Place the onions, garlic and other vegetables in an ovenproof dish and *drizzle* with olive oil. Add the rosemary and thyme.

3 Place on the middle shelf of the oven and *roast* for 20 minutes. Stir, *drizzle* over the honey and *roast* for another 20 minutes before serving.

Goes well with: Roast Chicken, page 156, Mango Lamb Chops, page 149, Honey Apple Chops, page 140

SIMPLE SIDES

SHOW-OFF RICE

Feeds 2
20 minutes

- 2 portions Basmati Rice (see recipe on page 98)
- 1 handful wild rice
- 1 teaspoon butter
- Salt and pepper
- Fresh chives for decoration (optional)

> This recipe is all about presentation. It's just a little bit different and jazzes up the usual dinner plate. Basmati rice contains slow-releasing starch and could help to keep your energy level more stable. Buy your rice in bulk to save money.

GO

1 Cook the basmati and wild rice separately. For instructions on cooking the basmati rice see page 98. To cook the wild rice, follow the instructions on the back of the packet.

2 When cooked through and still hot, mix the wild rice into the pan of basmati rice. Stir in the butter and add salt and pepper to taste.

3 Plate up and garnish with chopped chives or place an X made out of two chives on top.

Goes well with: Mango Lamb Chops, page 149, Roast Chicken, page 156, Baked Sweet Chilli Salmon, page 32, Lemon, Garlic and Herb Chicken, page 53

SPEEDY COUSCOUS SALAD

Feeds 2
10 minutes

GRAB

- 1 pack flavoured couscous
- Boiling water
- 1 red pepper, deseeded and chopped
- 1 red onion, peeled and finely chopped
- ¼ cucumber, *diced*
- ½ carrot, sliced
- 1 tablespoon olive oil

This is a great take-to-uni lunch and it costs next to nothing to make. Couscous is high in protein and low in calories - brilliant for when you're trying to get rid of a beer belly! It's dead easy to make and you can customise it with cooked meat, vegetables or even leftovers - go experiment!

GO

I Empty the packet of couscous into a bowl and add the amount of boiling water specified on the packet. Cover the top of the bowl with a plate and leave. When the couscous has soaked up all the liquid, fluff it up with a fork and set aside to cool.

2 Add the chopped pepper, onion, diced cucumber and sliced carrot to the cooled couscous with the olive oil. Stir and serve, or put into a small pot ready for the next time you need a snack over the next day or two.

Goes well with: Mango Lamb Chops, page 149, Best BBQ Wings, page 34

SPICY POTATO WEDGES

This recipe is cheaper than chips! The skin on a potato adds fibre, which helps you feel fuller for longer, as well as vitamin C – so keep the skins on!

Feeds 4
35 minutes

GRAB

- 4 large baking potatoes, cut into wedges
- 1 tablespoon olive oil
- 1 teaspoon mixed herbs
- 1 teaspoon chilli powder or paprika
- 1 teaspoon salt
- 1 teaspoon pepper
- Zip-lock bag

GO

1 Preheat the oven to 200°C/400°F/Gas Mark 6.

2 Pop the oil, herbs, spices, salt and pepper into a zip-lock bag and then add the wedges. Zip the bag up and shake until the wedges are covered, then tip out onto a baking tray covered in kitchen foil and bake in the preheated oven for 15 minutes.

3 Turn the wedges over with a wooden spatula and then bake for another 15 minutes. Leave in for another 5 minutes if you want very crispy wedges.

Goes well with: Best BBQ Wings, page 34, Sour Cream and Chive dip, page 87

STEAMED VEG

Feeds 2
5-10 minutes
3

GRAB

- Any three of the below:
- Broccoli, cut into *florets*
- Kale, sliced
- Carrots, peeled and sliced
- Potatoes, peeled and cut into chunks
- Sweet potatoes, peeled and cut into chunks
- Cauliflower, cut into *florets*
- Corn on the cob
- Mangetout
- Baby corn
- Green beans, trimmed
- Butternut squash, peeled and cut into chunks
- Brussel sprouts, trimmed
- Courgettes, ends cut off and cut into chunks

If you're having veg as a side or even a main dish, *steaming* it is the best way to preserve the nutritional value in the vegetable. Plus it means if you're sharing a kitchen you won't be hogging all the hob space. Test the vegetables by pricking with a fork to see if they are tender enough for your liking - but watch out for the steam!

GO

1 Fill the bottom of a three-tier steamer three-quarters full with water. Bring to the boil.

2 Put the potatoes in the water at the bottom of the steamer and then the leafier veggies at the top. Everything else you can put in the middle tier.

3 *Steam* the vegetables until they are firm but a knife slices through them easily. Serve while hot.

Goes well with: Roast Chicken, page 156, Lemon, Garlic and Herb Chicken, page 53, Sweet Chilli Salmon, page 32

STUFFED POTATO SKINS

Feeds 2
90 minutes

GRAB

- 2 large baking potatoes
- Small handful fresh chives or 2 spring onions, chopped
- Salt and pepper
- 1 teaspoon butter
- ½ mug grated cheese
- 1 tablespoon milk
- 2 rashers of bacon
- 1 teaspoon olive oil

If you're in a rush, just pierce each potato several times and cook in the microwave for about 8 minutes, turning halfway through cooking, then finish in the oven.

GO

1 Preheat the oven to 200°C/400°F/Gas Mark 6. Pierce the potatoes several times. Bake in the oven for 60 minutes turning them once.

2 Make a small cut in a potato and check to see if the inside is cooked – the knife should cut through easily. If not, put back in the oven for another 10 minutes.

3 When fully cooked, remove from the oven (leaving the oven on), cut the potatoes in half lengthways and spoon out the potato flesh, leaving just the skin so that it forms a 'shell'. Watch out for the steam that escapes from the potato – it's hot!

4 In a separate bowl, mash the potato flesh with the chives or spring onions, salt and pepper, butter and milk. Spoon the mixture back into the skins.

5 Chop the bacon finely and fry in the oil until crispy. Top the stuffed skins with a sprinkling of cheese and then the cooked bacon. Put back in the oven for 3 minutes or until the cheese is golden brown. When you've eaten the inside you can also eat the skins!

Goes well with: All-in Salad, page 93, Sour Cream and Chive dip, page 87

These are so tasty!
You can always trim the rind
and fat off the bacon to make it
lower in calories.

THREE VEG MASH

Feeds 4
30 minutes

GRAB

- 3 potatoes, peeled and *cubed*
- 2 sweet potatoes, peeled and *cubed*
- 3 carrots, peeled and *cubed*
- Salt and black pepper
- Squeeze of garlic puree (optional but compliments the sweetness of the mash)
- 1 teaspoon butter

Spice up your side of mash by using three (or more) types of vegetable and get more of your five a day. This is a great side recipe for novice cooks.

Try peeled and cubed butternut squash instead of carrots for a more savoury taste.

GO

1 Fill three pans or the bottom pan of a three-tier steamer halfway with water. Bring to the boil.

2 Distribute the vegetables between the three pans or tiers of the steamer.

3 Boil or *steam* the vegetables until they break up when you pierce them with a fork.

4 Place all of the cooked vegetables into a large bowl and add the salt, pepper, garlic puree and butter. Use a potato masher to break down the vegetables until they are light and fluffy —if you're in a rush put the whole lot in a blender and blend until smooth. Serve while hot.

SIMPLE SIDES

Goes well with: Lemon, Garlic and Herb Chicken, page 53, Roast Chicken, page 156, Mango Lamb Chops, page 149, Best BBQ Wings, page 34

TUNA AND SWEETCORN CHILLI PASTA

Feeds 1
10 minutes

Tuna is a really good source of protein. You will be using up so much energy studying and rushing around campus, so it is important to eat healthily throughout the day to keep your body and mind in optimum condition.

GRAB

- 1 tin of tuna
- ½ tin of sweetcorn
- 1 handful cooked pasta shapes
- 1 tablespoon low-fat mayonnaise
- 1 teaspoon chilli flakes

You can use the rest of the sweetcorn as a side, in a salad or in Chunky Veg Soup (see recipe on page 76).

GO

I Drain the tuna and sweetcorn and place a bowl. Stir in the cooked pasta, mayonnaise and chilli flakes. Enjoy!

 Goes well with: Baked Potato, page 31

TUNA NIÇOISE SALAD

GRAB

Feeds 1
20 minutes

- 2 eggs
- 1 large cooked potato, peeled and *diced*
- 1 yellow pepper, deseeded and chopped
- Handful rocket or mixed leaves
- Black olives (optional)
- 2 tomatoes, chopped
- 1 tin of tuna, drained
- Vinaigrette dressing (you can get this in the supermarket)

Replace tuna with salmon to get more fish oils into your diet and add a different flavour to the salad.

GO

1 Put the eggs in a pan of boiling water and cook for 6 minutes. Boil or *steam* the potato until soft.

2 Put the chopped pepper in a bowl and add the rocket or mixed leaves.

3 Add the cooked, diced potatoes and the olives if you like them. Peel and slice the eggs and place in the bowl along with the chopped tomatoes, then stir in the drained tuna and sprinkle over some vinaigrette dressing – done!

This is a handy recipe because you might already have the ingredients in your store cupboard or fridge. It's simple to make, and the potatoes, tuna and peppers are rich in iron, fibre and vitamins. If you feel like pushing the boat out, you could also replace the tinned tuna with grilled fresh tuna. This salad is cheaper than a cafeteria lunch and packs in the energy, protein and low-fat ingredients that could help you stay alert in lessons.

SMOOTHIES

BANANA, OAT AND HONEY SMOOTHIE

GRAB

- ¼ mug oatmeal
- 1 banana, peeled and chopped
- 1 tablespoon honey
- ½ mug milk
- 2 tablespoons natural yoghurt
- 1 teaspoon cinnamon (optional)

Feeds 1-2
5 minutes

> This gorgeous smoothie will help you to feel energised in the morning and full until break time. Oats are high in fibre, which is great for digestion. Try this smoothie if you have a long commute to uni.

GO

Dead easy – put everything in the blender, make sure the lid is on securely and blitz for 10 seconds or until smooth. Pour into a glass and enjoy.

If you don't have a blender you can just mash the chopped banana with a fork, put it in a jug with the other ingredients and whisk until thoroughly mixed.

SMOOTHIES

BLENDED ICED LATTE SMOOTHIE

GRAB

- 1 tablespoon freeze-dried coffee (Arabica and Robusta blend is best)
- 1 mug milk
- Handful of ice
- 1 teaspoon maple syrup
- 1 tablespoon vanilla ice cream

Make it mocha - add a tablespoon drinking chocolate.

Alternate with decaf coffee to keep your caffeine intake down.

GO

1 Put all the ingredients into a blender and blitz until smooth. Add more syrup to taste.

2 Pour into a glass and drink immediately.

Feeds 1
5 minutes

Caffeine has become part of the average student's life, even though trendy lattes and coffees from chain shops are hugely overpriced and often full of additives. It's important to watch your caffeine intake as too much can lead to heart problems - make your own coffees to keep track of how much you're drinking per week. You can make a simple iced latte yourself for less than 20% of the shop's price too!

FIVE-A-DAY FRESCO SMOOTHIE

GRAB

- Use five portions of fruit from the list below, e.g. 1 banana, 2 kiwis, 1 melon slice, 1 orange and 8 strawberries.
- 1 banana, peeled and sliced
- 8 strawberries, hulled
- 1 large slice melon, peeled and sliced
- 1 orange, peeled and segmented
- 1 handful raspberries
- 2 kiwi, peeled and sliced
- 6 pineapple chunks
- 2 satsumas, peeled and segmented
- 2 segments tinned peach
- 1 handful ice cubes or ½ mug apple juice

Feeds 3-4
10 minutes

I add a tablespoon natural yoghurt to my smoothie because I like the taste. You can add a small pot of flavoured yoghurt, honey or even raisins – 1 tablespoon raisins makes one of your five-a-day portions.

SMOOTHIES

GO

I Put the ice cubes in a blender with your choice of prepared fruit. Blitz in a blender until smooth. Serve immediately or keep in the fridge for up to 2 days.

Getting your five a day doesn't have to be a chore – you can get at least two in this smoothie. Sometimes as busy students we don't even have time to sit and munch an apple, so speed it up by using your blender to do the work for you. Smoothies are great to take with you to a study session or sports meet-up, and they're cheaper than an energy drink.

For more on five-a-day portions see: www.nhs.uk/Livewell/5ADAY

LIAM'S WAKE ME UP SMOOTHIE

GRAB

Feeds 3-4
5 minutes

- 1 handful strawberries, hulled
- 1 banana, peeled and sliced
- ½ an apple, quartered
- 1 glass orange juice
- 1 handful red grapes
- 3 ice cubes (optional)
- 1 teaspoon clear honey (optional)

Need an energy burst before a morning lecture? Grab this on your way out!

GO

1 Pour the orange juice into a blender along with the banana and blitz until smooth. Now add the rest of the fruit and the ice and blitz again for 10 seconds. If you want a sweeter smoothie, add the honey.

2 Pour into a glass and fuel up!

VERY BERRY SMOOTHIE

This smoothie is packed with vitamins and antioxidants that help keep cells healthy – great for the morning after! This is also a tasty treat to make for your family during the summer break.

GRAB

- 4 tablespoons vanilla or plain yoghurt
- ¼ pint milk
- Handful ice cubes
- Handful raspberries
- Handful strawberries, hulled
- Handful blackberries or blueberries
- 1 banana, peeled and sliced

Feeds 2
5 minutes

You can add 1 tablespoon clear honey if you'd like the smoothie sweeter. You can use frozen mixed berries and if you're lactose intolerant you can use soya milk and soya yoghurt.

GO

1 Put the fruit into a blender and spoon in the yoghurt, add the ice cubes and blend until smooth. Serve immediately or keep in the fridge for up to 2 days.

SMOOTHIES

SHARE THE LOVE

ADAM'S HOMEMADE BURGERS

GRAB

Feeds 4
40 minutes

- ½ an onion, peeled and very finely chopped
- 1 red chilli, finely chopped
- 1 teaspoon olive oil
- 1 egg
- 250g or 4 handfuls minced beef
- Salt and pepper
- ½ mug breadcrumbs (you can buy these or make your own in a food processor)
- 4 burger buns or small bread rolls

Toppings: Of course there are endless toppings for a burger beyond a slice of cheese and some bacon - a slice of beetroot and a fried egg is nice, as are onion rings or a hash brown. You could also add salsa or chutney.

GO

1 Peel and very finely chop the onion (or blitz in a food processor). Remove the stalk end from the chilli if you're using it, fry the chopped onion and chilli in a teaspoon of olive oil until soft, then set aside to cool. Crack the egg into a mug and whisk with a fork.

2 In a separate bowl, season the minced beef with salt and pepper, then add the breadcrumbs, onion, chilli and egg.

3 With clean hands or disposable gloves, mix the ingredients together and form into burger shapes by rolling into medium-sized balls and flattening. Fry the burgers in a little olive oil for 4–5 minutes on either side, turning once to ensure that they are fully cooked. Check by piercing with a knife – the juices should run clear.

4 Put each burger into a bun, add your desired toppings and eat. You can also toast the buns under the grill on a low heat just to crisp them up.

 Goes well with: Spiced Potato Wedges, page 118

SHARE THE LOVE

Buying burgers frozen or from fast-food restaurants could mean that you are taking in many additives and chemicals. Making your own burgers is cheaper and you are using fresh ingredients, which is better for you in the long run, especially when you're trying to maintain a healthy lifestyle.

BRUSCHETTA

Feeds 4
30 minutes

GRAB

- 1 pack of cherry tomatoes, quartered
- 1 red onion, peeled and finely chopped
- 1 teaspoon dried mixed herbs
- 2 tablespoon olive oil
- 2 tablespoons balsamic vinegar
- 1 tablespoon honey
- Salt and black pepper
- Loaf of French bread or large ciabatta

Change up your toppings: try torn mozzarella, basil and a drizzle of olive oil; red pesto, torn mozzarella and sliced olives; grated parmesan cheese, rocket and chopped sun-dried tomatoes; cubed feta cheese and chopped mixed herbs; cubed goat's cheese and sliced red onion.

Good for sharing and quick to make, bruschetta also contains one of the sometimes hard to fit in five a day. The lutein in tomatoes is an antioxidant that helps to maintain muscle tissues, for example in the eyes. Bruschetta is simple to make but looks impressive – serve it up at the weekend after a week of hard work.

SHARE THE LOVE

GO

I Place the quartered tomatoes in a small mixing bowl with the finely chopped red onion. Add the mixed herbs, 1 tablespoon olive oil, balsamic vinegar and honey and stir well. Season with salt and pepper. Cover the bowl with cling film or foil and place in the fridge for 30 minutes.

2 Cut the ciabatta or French stick into slices and *drizzle* with olive oil. Place face down on a griddle pan to cook for 10 minutes, then place on a plate.

3 Spoon the tomato mixture onto the toasted bread and *drizzle* the prepared juices over the top. Add other toppings as desired.

COCONUT, CHILLI AND KING PRAWN CURRY

DR OPARA'S FOOD FOR THOUGHT
Your body can only run on what it's given
so feed it well. You can't concentrate when
you're hungry.

Feeds 2
30 minutes

GRAB

- 2 tablespoons olive oil
- 1 onion, peeled and finely chopped
- 2 cloves garlic, finely chopped
- 1 red chilli, deseeded and finely chopped
- 2 tablespoons fresh coriander leaves, finely chopped
- 400ml coconut milk
- 1 pack cooked jumbo or king prawns, defrosted if frozen
- 1 teaspoon sugar

If you don't have fresh chillies or coriander you can use chilli flakes and dried coriander instead, but fresh ingredients give the curry a more authentic flavour.

GO

I   Heat the olive oil in a saucepan. Add the chopped onion, garlic and red chilli, and cook until soft over a medium heat.

2   Add the chopped coriander to the onion mixture and cook together for 2 more minutes. Pour over the coconut milk and sugar, then add the prawns and stir. *Simmer* for about 5 minutes until hot.

Goes well with: Basmati Rice, page 98

Prawns can be a
great source of protein,
especially if you don't eat much
red meat. They're a bit expensive, but
this recipe is great when you want to
enjoy something a little special
on date night.

EASY SHARING WRAPS

Feeds as many as you need!
10 minutes

GRAB

- Tomatoes, sliced
- Lettuce, torn
- 1–2 plain flour tortillas per person
- Chopped cooked meat, tofu or veggies of your choice
- Garlic salt and black pepper (optional)
- Salsa (see recipe on page 86)
- Sour Cream and Chive dip (see recipe on page 87)

GO

1 Heat the tortillas under the grill or in the microwave for about 10 seconds – sprinkle with a few drops of water before warming to stop them drying out.

2 Lay a few pieces of the meat, tofu or veg on the tortilla. Lay the torn lettuce and sliced tomatoes on top of that. Add garlic salt and black pepper to season if you like. Pile on a teaspoon of salsa or sour cream and chive dip, or more according to taste.

3 Fold one half up so you have a semi-circular shape. Now fold the sides in on each other so your tortilla filling is safely held within them and doesn't fall out!

Wraps are a very easy way to use up leftovers and get carbs, protein and vegetables all in one go. You can use tofu instead of meat to make your meal less expensive and veggie friendly. You'll need about 1 tomato, 2 lettuce leaves and a handful of meat, veg or tofu per person. Wraps are a good sharing meal, a great start when getting to know your new buddies in halls.

HONEY APPLE CHOPS

Feeds as many as you need!
35 minutes (+ marinating)

Pork is a good source
of protein, which helps
to maintain muscle. Select lean
pork chops to reduce your fat intake.
Meat can be expensive, so put your money
together for those 'buy one get one free' or
'3 for £10' deals, then split the selection and
freeze any extra until you need it. These
chops also make a really tasty sandwich
when combined with thick slices
of crusty bread.

GRAB

- 1 tablespoon apple sauce per person
- 1 tablespoon clear honey per person
- ½ teaspoon black pepper per person
- 1 boneless pork chop per person

GO

1 Put the apple sauce in a bowl, add the honey and pepper and mix well. Make 3 *scores* on each chop to enable the meat to soak up the sauce. Place the chops in a large bowl and use your hands to smear the marinade mixture in to make sure the chops are well covered. Leave for at least 30 minutes.

2 Place the chops into a kitchen foil-lined baking dish. Grill under a medium heat until the chops are golden brown, turning over once.

Goes well with: Roasted Veg Medley, page 112, Steamed Veg, page 119, Three Veg Mash, page 122, Black Pepper Mash, page 100, Easy Cook Rice, page 98, Show-Off Rice, page 114 Speedy Couscous Salad, page 116

JULIA'S BACON, LEEK AND LAGER RISOTTO

Risotto makes a good meal when you're on a tight budget but want to eat something filling and fresh. Adding lager instead of wine intensifies the mild flavour of the leeks. Leeks are part of the garlic and onion family, and share some of their anti-bacterial properties. They also contain Vitamin A, which can help with the production of white blood cells. Risotto looks hard to make but it really isn't - tackle it with a friend the first few times and learn together.

Feeds 2
40 minutes

GRAB

- 1 teaspoon butter
- 1 teaspoon olive oil
- 2 leeks, sliced
- 2 handfuls or 150g risotto rice
- ½ litre chicken stock
- ½ litre lager (or use 1 litre chicken stock if you'd rather)
- 3 rashers cooked bacon, chopped
- 1 handful button mushrooms, chopped
- Salt and pepper to season

Pimp your risotto! Add a dash of cream, chopped fresh herbs or a sprinkle of Cheddar or Parmesan cheese or top with a poached egg.

GO

1 Melt the butter in a medium-sized frying pan, then add the olive oil, tilting the pan so that the oils cover the base. *Sauté* the chopped leeks for 5 minutes.

2 Add the risotto rice and cook for 2–3 minutes until the grains become translucent. Pour over half the lager or stock, let it *simmer* for 3 minutes, then add the chopped cooked bacon and chopped mushrooms.

3 Carefully add the rest of the lager and chicken stock, one ladle at a time. Keep stirring until the rice has absorbed the liquid, then repeat. This can take up to 20–30 minutes so be patient – the rice is ready when it still has a slight 'bite' to it.

4 Add the salt and pepper, then plate up and tuck in.

LARRY'S CHILLI CON CARNE

Feeds 4
30 minutes

GRAB

- 500g minced beef
- 1 teaspoon tomato puree
- 1 teaspoon garlic puree
- ½ onion, peeled and chopped
- 2 tomatoes, chopped
- 3 mushrooms, chopped
- 1 red chilli or ½ Scotch bonnet chilli, deseeded and chopped – or use 1 teaspoon Helen's Hot Pepper Sauce (see recipe on page 88)
- 1 tablespoon olive oil
- 400g tin kidney beans
- Sun-dried tomato puree (optional)

You can add tinned sweetcorn, cooked and cubed butternut squash, more mushrooms or a chopped green pepper to add more bulk if you haven't got enough meat or would like to make a vegetarian version.

GO

1 Put a large non-stick frying pan on a medium heat. When hot, add the mince and purees and stir. Seal the meat by *browning* it until cooked and then place the mixture in a bowl.

2 Add the chopped onion, tomatoes, mushrooms and chilli (if using) to the pan with a tablespoon of oil and fry for about 3–4 minutes or until the vegetables start to soften.

3 Return the meat back to the pan with the vegetables. Drain the kidney beans in a colander or sieve, rinse them under the cold tap, stir them into the meat mixture on a high heat and then *simmer* for a further 10 minutes. If you're using hot pepper sauce, add it now. If you feel the sauce isn't thick enough, stir in a squirt of sun-dried tomato puree.

Literally meaning 'chilli and meat', Chilli con Carne is easy to make with friends and stores well in the fridge, or you can cool and freeze it to eat later. As for the kidney beans, the whole tin makes up one of your five a day – perfect!

Goes well with: Easy Sharing Wraps, page 138, Easy Cook Rice, page 98, Baked Potato, page 31, Three Veg Mash, page 122

LASAGNE

Lasagne is one of those comforting meals that tastes delicious with almost any side dish and it's easy to make with friends after work. You can even eat it the next day for lunch. Cheap mince can contain a lot of fat, so try using turkey mince or Quorn for a healthier option.

Feeds 4-6
40 minutes

GRAB

- 1 onion, peeled and finely chopped
- 2 cloves garlic, peeled and finely chopped
- Butter
- 500g or three handfuls minced meat (normally beef; you can use fresh or frozen)
- Black pepper
- 1 tablespoon tomato ketchup
- 1 tablespoon dried mixed herbs
- Handful mushrooms, sliced

- 1 carrot, grated
- 1 portion Red Sauce (see recipe on page 90)
- About 9 egg pasta lasagne sheets
- 1 portion White Sauce (see recipe on page 91)
- Grated Cheddar cheese or a handful of torn mozzarella

For vegetarian option replace the meat with Quorn or a thick vegetable like sliced aubergine, cut lengthways or sliced tomatoes. For a vegan option replace meat with tofu, a handful of frozen spinach and use vegan friendly lasagne sheets and cheese substitute.

GO

1 Preheat the oven to 200°C/400°F/Gas Mark 6.

2 Melt a knob of butter in a medium saucepan over a low heat. Add the chopped onion and garlic to the pan. When soft, add the minced meat.

3 When the meat has *browned*, drain the meat juices and add black pepper, ketchup and the mixed herbs. Add the sliced mushrooms and grated carrot to the pan. Pour in the red sauce and stir until all ingredients are covered. Cover with a lid and *simmer* on a low heat for 5 minutes.

4 When that's done, pour a third of the contents of the pan into a lasagne dish, layer a third of the lasagne sheets over the meat to cover it all, then layer a third of the white sauce on top of that.

5 Repeat step 4 twice more and then sprinkle the grated cheese or torn mozzarella on top of all of that. Dish size and layer thickness may vary, so learn as you go!

6 Cook the lasagne in the oven for 30–40 minutes. When the cheese is golden brown on top, remove the lasagne and rest it on the side for one minute.

Goes well with: Steamed Veg, page 119, Homemade Garlic Bread, page 106

LIPSTICK PUNCH

- Pack of strawberries
- Fresh fruit – grapes, orange slices, apple slices, melon slices
- Ice cubes
- 2 pints red grape juice
- 1 pint cranberry juice
- 1 pint apple juice (or orange juice)
- 1 pint soda
- 1 pint vodka

Feeds 6
40 minutes

Try using peach schnapps instead of vodka, or for a non-alcoholic version skip the alcohol and leave the punch fresh and fruity.

GO

1 Remove the green tops from the strawberries and discard, then chop up the strawberries and blitz in a blender until smooth. If you don't have a blender, just use a potato masher to turn the fruit into a pulp, then a spoon to push that through a sieve.

2 Grab a large bowl and add ice cubes until it's half full. Add all the juices, soda and alcohol, and stir well.

3 Leave to chill in the fridge for about 20 minutes, then add the sliced fresh fruit and blended strawberries – and ladle into glasses!

We all know that fresh fruit is good for our bodies, giving us natural sugar, energy and vitamins. With punch you can add as many fruits as you like, but don't add too much alcohol as the flavours of the fruit will be overpowered and you may end up going over your recommended alcohol units!

MANGO LAMB CHOPS

Feeds 2
20 minutes

GRAB

- 2 lamb chops
- 2 garlic cloves, sliced (alternatively you can rub a sprinkle of garlic salt into each chop)
- Jar of mango chutney
- Basmati rice to serve

GO

1 Place the lamb chops on a kitchen foil-lined baking tray. Make small incisions in the chop and press the sliced garlic into them. Drop about a teaspoon of mango chutney onto each chop and smear it evenly across the top.

2 Place the chops under a hot grill for 5–8 minutes. They cook very quickly, so stay by them to make sure they don't burn. *Baste* them in the juices that come out of the chops and turn them over at least once.

3 When the chops are a nice brown colour and the fat is crispy, put a little more chutney on each one and turn the grill up to maximum so that the chutney caramelises.

Lamb is high in protein, which is essential for muscle growth and repair. It also contains iron, which is essential for the delivery of oxygen to your cells. Good-quality lamb chops can be pricey, so enjoy this recipe on special occasions.

This dish is quite sweet, so it's good served with plain basmati rice.

Goes well with: Basmati Rice, page 98, Black Pepper Mash, page 100, Roasted Veg Medley, page 112, Steamed Veg, page 119

SHARE THE LOVE

MELANZANE

Feeds 4
45 minutes

GRAB

- 1 aubergine, sliced thinly
- Olive oil
- 1 onion, peeled and *diced*
- 1 tomato, sliced
- 1 can chopped tomatoes
- 1 teaspoon cinnamon
- 2 cloves garlic, *crushed*
- 1 teaspoon tomato puree
- Grated cheese or torn mozzarella

The Italians know it as the 'crazy apple', but the aubergine is actually nutritious and low in fat. It is also rich in vitamin C, which may help to boost your immune system. Definitely a sharing recipe!

GO

1 Preheat the oven to 180°C/350°F/Gas Mark 4.

2 Brush the sliced aubergine with oil and cook on a heated griddle or frying pan until slightly wilted and browned.

3 Cook the diced onion with the sliced tomato in a saucepan. When the onions go soft, add the chopped tomatoes, cinnamon, salt and pepper, garlic and tomato puree. Stir and *simmer* over a low heat for 10 minutes.

4 In an ovenproof dish, spoon a layer of sauce on the bottom and layer with grated cheese or thinly sliced/torn mozzarella, then add enough disks of aubergine to cover the layer underneath. Repeat the layering until all the ingredients are used up, then top with cheese.

5 Bake in the oven for 30 minutes, until the cheese is brown.

 Goes well with: Homemade Garlic Bread, page 106

MINI MOVIE PIZZAS

Feeds 4
40 minutes

GRAB

- Pack of mini pitta breads
- Toppings – sliced ham and pepperoni/ sliced red onion and tinned sweetcorn/torn mozzarella and halved cherry tomatoes/grated cheddar and chopped spinach/sliced roast chicken and BBQ sauce

Why not try using chopped anchovies or olives for a real taste of Italy?

These mini pizzas are a cheaper and healthier alternative to takeaway pizzas. You can add more fresh vegetables and control the amount of sauce or cheese you are using, lowering your fat intake and adding more nutrients to your diet. This is one of my favourite sharing recipes - everyone bring an ingredient or two, get the oven or grill on and have fun creating together.

GO

1 Preheat the oven to 150°C/300°F/Gas Mark 2.

2 Lightly toast the pittas in the oven on a kitchen foil-covered baking tray (foil stops the toppings baking onto the tray and becoming solid!). Toasting the pittas first helps them hold the weight of the toppings.

3 Remove the tray from the oven and add your chosen toppings to the pittas carefully.

4 Place the topped pittas back in the oven and bake (or put under a medium grill) until the cheese is golden and the meats are crispy.

5 Leave to cool down a bit, then tuck in.

Goes well with: Homemade Garlic Bread, page 106, All-in Salad, page 93, Spicy Potato Wedges, page 118

PINK PANTHER

Feeds 6
30 minutes

GRAB

- 2 handfuls fresh or frozen raspberries
- 2 handfuls ice cubes
- 1 bottle lemonade
- 1 lime, sliced
- 6 glasses

Add ½ a shot of vodka or Sambuca to each glass to make a tasty, refreshing cocktail.

GO

1 Blend the raspberries and ice cubes until smooth.

2 Fill glasses halfway with the fruit mixture, then top up with lemonade and garnish with a half slice of lime.

Raspberries are high in antioxidants, which help to promote cell health. Adding fruit to your drinks increases their health benefit, even if it's just a handful! This looks good and is alcohol free - great for detoxing or relaxing.

SHARE THE LOVE

PUFF PASTRY PIZZA

Feeds 4
35 minutes

- 1 sheet puff pastry
- 2 tablespoon of tomato puree
- Tablespoon red or green pesto
- Olive oil
- 1 ball of mozzarella, sliced
- Cherry tomatoes, halved
- Fresh basil or spinach, torn (if you don't have fresh herbs you can use dried mixed herbs)

Try adding some chopped cooked bacon or pepperoni to the topping for extra flavour.

GO

1 Preheat the oven to 220°C/425°F/Gas Mark 7.

2 Unroll the sheet of puff pastry and place it on a baking tray lined with greaseproof paper. Smooth on the tomato puree and pesto, leave a 2cm border (about the width of the tip of your thumb) – this makes it easier for the edges to rise. Brush the border with olive oil to give it a golden colour as it cooks.

3 Place the mozzarella and tomatoes evenly across the pastry.

4 Sprinkle over the herbs and place in the preheated oven for 15–20 minutes, or until the cheese has melted and is golden brown. Using a spatula, lift the pastry gently to check that the bottom isn't soggy or pale. If it is, pop back in the oven for another 5 minutes or until crisp.

Goes well with: All-in Salad, page 93

Puff pastry pizzas
are quick to make and
are great for sharing. The fresh
vegetable toppings can help boost
your immunity level.

ROAST CHICKEN

Feeds 4+
80 minutes

Roast chicken is a great student meal because it's quick and easy, but most importantly the chicken provides a lot of protein. You can also use the leftover chicken in lots of different recipes.

GRAB

- 1 small chicken (1–1.5kg)
- 1 lemon
- 1 tablespoon butter
- Salt and pepper to season

GO

1 Preheat the oven to 190°C/375°F/Gas Mark 5. Pierce several holes in the breast of the chicken. Cut the lemon in half and squeeze the juice all over the top of the chicken. Put the lemon halves into the cavity. Season with salt and pepper and rub butter all over the skin – don't forget the wings!

2 Put the chicken in a kitchen foil-lined roasting tin. Turn the chicken upside down so that the breast will soak up all the juices as it *roasts*. Put in the centre of the oven – *baste* at least three times during *roasting*. Calculate the cooking time at 45 minutes per kilo plus 20 minutes, so a small chicken will take 65–85 minutes.

3 Make sure the chicken is cooked by sticking a skewer or fork into the leg joint –the juices should run clear, with no sign of pinkness in the meat. Remember, the bigger the chicken, the longer you have to *roast* it.

4 When the chicken is completely cooked, leave to stand for 10 minutes, then slice off enough for the current meal. Cool the remaining chicken and refrigerate in a plastic lidded container for up to two days.

Goes well with: Three Veg Mash, page 122, Roasted Veg Medley, page 112, Steamed Veg, page 119

Serve with new potatoes and gravy for extra tastiness – I just use gravy granules, as they're quick and simple.

TEQUILA LEMONADE

Feeds 4-6
10 minutes

GRAB

- 1 bottle tequila
- 1 bottle still lemonade
- 1 lime, sliced
- 1 lemon, sliced
- 1 teaspoon ginger, grated (optional)

Tequila is known best as a main component of shots, but it can be combined with lemonade to make a refreshing and less alcoholic drink - a better option if you like tequila but not hangovers!

GO

1 Pour half a pint of tequila into a large jug. Add 3 pints of still lemonade and stir well.

2 Add the sliced lemon and lime to the jug, together with the grated ginger if you like. Pop in the fridge to chill. Serve with ice cubes and add slices of the fruit to the glass.

THAI GREEN CHICKEN CURRY

Feeds 4
30 minutes

GRAB

- 1 tablespoon olive oil
- 1 tin coconut milk
- 2 tablespoons Thai green curry paste
- Pack of four chicken breasts, cubed
- 1 tablespoon coconut cream
- 2 small red chillies, deseeded and chopped
- Half a mug mangetout
- Half a mug baby sweetcorn
- Small handful fresh coriander, finely chopped

The fresh ingredients in this curry mean that you could be getting more nutrients than a pre-packaged ready meal. Instead of going out and spending your cash on extras, make this tasty meal at home and have date night in.

GO

1   Heat the oil in a deep frying pan and add ¼ of the tin of coconut milk. Spoon in the curry paste and stir until both ingredients are blended.

2   Add the chicken cubes to the pan. Stir until the chicken is covered in the sauce. Add the rest of the coconut milk, the coconut cream, the chopped chillies and the vegetables. Cook on a high heat until bubbling then *simmer* for a further 10 minutes until the chicken is cooked.

3   Stir in the chopped coriander and leave on a low heat for 4 minutes before serving.

Goes well with: Basmati Rice, page 98

VODKA JELLY SHOTS

Of course I'm going to say drink responsibly and always keep track of how many units you're consuming - trying to complete an assignment with a hangover isn't fun! There is one good thing about small quantities of vodka, as opposed to the typical student tipple of beer: vodka is very low in carbohydrates, whereas beer can add to weight gain, as we know from the term 'beer belly'.

For tropical flavour vodka jellies try mixing strawberry, orange and lime jelly cubes together. Create layered jelly shots by making up three different flavours of jelly and then adding a layer at a time into the shot glass allowing the jelly to set before adding another layer. Lemon, strawberry and orange work well together.

Feeds 20
6 hours (including chilling)

GRAB

- 1 packet any flavour jelly cubes
- Boiling water
- About 15–20 shot glasses or plastic shot-sized cups
- Bottle of vodka

GO

1 Break up the jelly cubes and put them in a large bowl. Add the amount of boiling water stated on the jelly packet and stir until all the cubes have broken down and dissolved. You should be left with a coloured liquid.

2 Pour the liquid into shot glasses until they are about 80% full. Leave to cool for 5 minutes, then top each up with 2 tablespoons vodka. Don't add the vodka while the jelly liquid is still boiling hot, as the alcohol will evaporate!

3 When all the glasses are full, place on a tray and leave to set in the fridge for at least 5–6 hours, or overnight if possible.

VODKA SALMON PASTA

Feeds 2
30 minutes

GRAB

- 2 salmon fillets
- Olive oil
- 2 handfuls pasta
- 1 red onion, finely chopped
- 2 cloves garlic, finely chopped
- Tin chopped tomatoes
- 1 squirt tomato puree
- 200ml single cream
- 1 shot vodka

You can use different types of pasta shapes or linguine with this dish and even skip the alcohol to make a non-alcoholic, milder version.

GO

1 Preheat the oven to 150°C/300°F/Gas Mark 2.

2 *Drizzle* the salmon fillets with olive oil and wrap loosely in kitchen foil. Place in the oven and cook for 15 minutes.

3 Bring a large pan of water to the boil and cook the pasta for 2 minutes, then turn down and *simmer* until *al dente*. Drain and set aside.

4 Heat a splash of oil in a large frying pan and *sauté* the chopped onion and garlic until soft.

5 Add the chopped tomatoes and puree to the pan, and *simmer* on a low heat for 5 minutes. Add the cream and vodka to the mixture and stir in, then *simmer* for another 10 minutes. Pop the pasta into the pan and stir it into the sauce.

6 When the salmon is cooked through, allow it to cool then use a fork to flake the flesh or tear it into chunks. Add the fish to the sauce and stir again.

7 Plate up and enjoy!

Salmon is a really good source of Omega 3 fatty acids. Although it's pricey it makes a good meal, especially for date night or cooking for your family back home.

DR OPARA'S FOOD FOR THOUGHT
I acknowledge it's not always easy to sort out an evening meal if you're on campus, but if you live nearby or are studying in halls you and your friends can take turns to cook.

SWEET TREATS

CHOCO RICE CRISPY CAKES

Feeds 20
10 minutes

GRAB

- 1 large chocolate bar or two Mars bars
- 1 teaspoon butter
- ½ mug mini marshmallows plus some for decoration (optional)
- 2 mugs Rice Crispies
- 2 cupcake trays and cake cases (or line a cake tin with greaseproof paper or foil then pour the mixture into it and cut into squares after it's cooled)

You can use chocolate Rice Crispies instead of plain to make the treats even more chocolatey.

These cakes are easy to make and lower in fat than cupcakes piled high with icing. They're good for a club meet-up or having friends round when you want a speedy, cheap dessert.

SWEET TREATS

GO

1 Break up the chocolate bar/Mars bars in a medium bowl and add the butter. Microwave on a low heat setting for about 1½ minutes. Watch to see when the chocolate has melted and make sure that it doesn't bubble or burn.

2 Stir in the marshmallows and a handful of Rice Crispies. When these are completely covered by the chocolate, add more Rice Crispies according to how much sauce you have, until the Rice Crispies have a thin covering of chocolate and there isn't any sauce at the bottom of the bowl.

3 Put the cake cases into the tray holes. Using a tablespoon, fill them with the mixture and top with a mini marshmallow if you like.

4 Leave to set until hard. You can serve these straight away or store in an airtight container for up to two days.

CLASSIC FRUIT SALAD

Feeds 2
10 minutes

- 1 kiwi, peeled and chopped
- 1 orange, peeled and segmented
- A small bunch of grapes
- 4 strawberries, hulled and halved
- 1 apple, sliced and cored
- Lemon juice (optional)

GO

I Add all of your prepared fruit into a bowl. Enjoy!

Eat the fruit salad as it is with a spoon or divide into smaller pots for on-the-go snacks.

Steer clear of the vending machine and save money by choosing fresh fruit as a snack. It's good for keeping your immune system and energy levels topped up when leading a busy student life.

You can add a little lemon juice to stop the apple going brown.

DANIKA'S CHOCOLATE BROWNIES

Feeds 6
50 minutes

GRAB

- 400g milk or dark chocolate
- 200g butter plus some to grease the tray with
- 3 medium eggs
- 225g light Muscovado sugar
- 2 teaspoons vanilla extract
- 30g cocoa powder
- 85g self-raising flour
- Handful pecans or hazelnuts, chopped, plus some for decoration (optional)
- 20cm baking tin

Serve the brownies with a scoop of ice cream or fresh raspberries as a garnish.

GO

1 Preheat the oven to 160°C/325°F/Gas Mark 3.

2 Break the chocolate into small pieces in a heatproof bowl. Place the bowl on top of a medium pan of *simmering* water, ensuring that the bottom of the bowl doesn't touch the water. Leave the chocolate to melt and then stir in the butter until dissolved. Remove the bowl from the pan.

3 Crack the eggs into a separate bowl and *beat* in the sugar and vanilla extract. Now pour in the chocolate and add the cocoa powder, pecans or chopped hazelnuts and stir thoroughly with a wooden spoon.

4 Grease the baking tin with butter and line with greaseproof paper. Pour the mixture in and, if you like, sprinkle a few pecans or hazelnuts on top. Bake in the oven for at least 30 minutes or until the surface is set and the brownies begin to come away from the sides of the baking tin.

5 Remove from the oven and set aside until completely cold – then turn out, remove the greaseproof paper and enjoy!

Chocolate doesn't have to be unhealthy – it's all about eating it in moderation. Indulge after finishing your last essay before the holidays, or you could even make these and box some up as a gift for a friend.

FUNDRAISER FAIRY CAKES

Feeds more than 12
40 minutes

Fairy cakes are brilliant because they're cheap to make and are just enough of a treat. When I was doing revision I found that these cakes helped me perk up a bit and also made fun little surprises. They will also attract lots of students to your fundraising table or society at the Freshers Fair!

GRAB

- 175g caster sugar (normal sugar will also work; 12 tablespoons)
- 175g butter (12 tablespoons)
- 3 eggs
- 1 teaspoon vanilla essence
- 175g self-raising flour (12 tablespoons)
- Cupcake tray and cake cases

GO

1 Put a paper cake case into each hole on the cupcake tray, make sure the cases aren't doubled up. Preheat the oven to 180°C/350°F/Gas Mark 4.

2 Spoon the sugar into a large bowl and add the butter. *Cream* the butter and sugar together until pale in colour and fluffy. Crack the eggs into a mug and *beat* with a fork. Using a large wooden spoon, stir the eggs into the butter and sugar a bit at a time. Add the vanilla essence.

3 Now spoon in the flour and scoop the mixture on top of it until the flour is covered (if you have an electric whisk you can use this instead on a low setting). Stir gently until all the mixture is blended smoothly.

4 Using a metal tablespoon, drop a heaped spoonful of the mixture into each cake case. Bake the cakes on the middle shelf of the oven for about 20 minutes. Poke a knife into the middle of a few cakes after 15 minutes – if the blade comes out clean then the cakes are ready. If you don't want to cut the cakes you can just tap the top of the cakes gently – if they spring back they are ready. Remove from the oven and leave to cool before decorating with buttercream or icing.

You can top your cakes with the buttercream recipe given with Mum's Victoria Sponge Cake on page 174. Or simply follow the instructions on the back of a box of icing sugar, adding a dash of food colouring to jazz up your cakes.

LAUREN'S SWEET FRUIT SALAD

Feeds 3-4
5 minutes

GRAB

- Handful strawberries, hulled and sliced
- Handful seedless red grapes
- ½ Cantaloupe melon, peeled and *cubed*

GO

1 Put all of your prepared fruit into a large plastic box.

Store in a covered container in the fridge for up to 3 days.

> This fruit salad is one of my favourites, and is really quick to make. Fruit salad can be a refreshing treat after a long summer's day finishing off last-minute work and finding all your library books!

DR OPARA'S FOOD FOR THOUGHT
Reading for a degree is hard work
so you need proper sustenance.

MUM'S VICTORIA SPONGE CAKE

Using a lower-fat butter substitute will keep the calories down – plus it's easier to cream than real butter! Adding fresh raspberries to the filling could give you a small dose of Vitamin C and antioxidants. Once you get the hang of baking you'll be able to make birthday cakes for friends or for fundraising events.

Feeds 6
45 minutes

GRAB

- 175g butter or lower-fat substitute (12 tablespoons) plus some to grease the cake tins with
- 175g caster sugar (normal sugar will also work; 12 tablespoons)
- 3 eggs
- 175g self-raising flour (12 tablespoons)
- 1 teaspoon vanilla essence
- Two 25cm cake tins
- For the filling:
- 85g butter or lower-fat substitute (6 tablespoons)
- 175g icing sugar (12 tablespoons)
- 2 tablespoons jam – strawberry or raspberry works best
- 8 whole fresh raspberries or 8 halved strawberries

You can make this cake with gluten-free or brown rice flour, just add 1 teaspoon gluten-free baking powder along with it.

GO

1 Preheat the oven to 180°C/350°F/Gas Mark 4. Smear a teaspoon of butter around the cake tins and line with greaseproof paper.

2 *Cream* the butter and sugar together with a wooden spoon or mixer until light and fluffy.

3 Break the eggs into a mug and *beat* with a fork. Stir into the butter and sugar in three stages, mixing well between each stage. Sift in the flour and stir in gently. Add the vanilla essence.

4 Split the mixture between the two greased tins and bake in the oven for about 25 minutes. Poke a knife through the middle – if it comes out clean the cakes are ready. Turn the cakes out of the tins and cool on a wire rack.

5 To make the buttercream filling, *beat* the butter until smooth and then sift in the icing sugar in four stages, mixing well between each stage.

6 Now spread the flat side of one of the cakes with a layer of jam and the other with the buttercream filling. Add the fruit to the bottom layer if using, then squish the layers together. Sift some icing sugar over the top, slice and serve.

MY GRANNIE'S FLAPJACKS

Feeds 12
40 minutes

Grannies have the best recipes! I love these moist, chewy flapjacks - especially with the coconut. They store well, so if you're in a rush you can just grab a few squares to keep you full until break. Put some in a box and decorate with ribbon to make a cute gift at Christmas or a birthday.

GRAB

- 250g unsalted butter
- 5 tablespoons clear honey
- 170g light muscovado sugar
- Juice of ½ lemon
- 340g porridge oats
- Large non-stick baking tray
- Greaseproof paper

You can add ½ mug desiccated coconut, dried cranberries and raisins, dates or other fruit and nuts. You can even dip them in melted chocolate if you like.

GO

1 Preheat the oven to 180°C/350°F/Gas Mark 4.

2 Put a large pan over a low heat. *Cube* the butter, add to the pan and melt gently. Spoon in the honey and then the sugar and stir.

3 Now squeeze the juice from the lemon – minus pips – into the saucepan and stir again. Add any coconut, fruit or nuts that you want to use.

4 Add the porridge oats and stir in well with a wooden spoon.

5 Line a large non-stick baking tray with greaseproof paper and pour the mixture into it, spreading evenly with the back of a wooden spoon. Using a sharp knife, *score* into 12 even squares (don't slice right through). Scoring them now will make the flapjacks easier to cut into squares when they're cooked!

6 Put the tray in the middle of the oven for 15 minutes. Turn the tray around and bake for another 10 minutes.

7 When the flapjacks are cooked, remove from the oven, gently *score* the lines again and leave to cool. When cooled, cut into squares. You can store the flapjacks in a tin or airtight container for up to 1 week.

8 If you want to, melt half a bar of milk chocolate, add a teaspoon of milk, stir and then dip one side of the cooked and cooled flapjack in it, and leave to set on a flat tray.

MY SISTER'S BANANA MUFFINS

Feeds 6
40 minutes

GRAB

- 250g self-raising flour (16 level tablespoons)
- 1 teaspoon baking powder
- ½ teaspoon bicarbonate of soda
- Pinch of salt
- 1 teaspoon ground ginger
- 75g butter (1 heaped tablespoon)
- 120ml milk (half a mug)
- 2 eggs
- 2 large ripe bananas, peeled and mashed
- 2 tablespoons clear honey
- Optional additions: 1 teaspoon cinnamon, 1 teaspoon nutmeg, 1 small carrot, grated
- Muffin/cupcake tray and muffin cases

Serve with vanilla ice cream or fresh cream (optional).

Bananas are high in potassium, which can help maintain brain function. Shop-bought muffins are notoriously high in fat and additives, so bake them at home and also benefit from saving money. Not only will these muffins make your kitchen smell amazing, they taste even better! When baking it's important to use precise measurements, but I've given approximate equivalents in case you don't have a set of scales.

GO

1 Preheat the oven to 190°C/175°F/Gas Mark 5 and line the muffin tray with cases. Sift the flour, baking powder, bicarbonate of soda, salt and ginger into a bowl. If you want to include cinnamon or nutmeg, add that now too.

2 Melt the butter in a plastic jug in the microwave for 20 seconds and set aside to cool.

3 Add the milk and eggs to the flour, then mix thoroughly with a spoon. Mash the bananas and add into the mixture, with the grated carrot if you like. Pour in the melted butter and the honey and mix with a wooden spoon or electric mixer until combined.

4 Transfer the mixture into a jug and pour into the muffin cases until each is three-quarters full. Bake for 25 minutes. Use a skewer to pierce the muffins – if the skewer comes out clean they are ready.

NO EGG COOKIE STARS

Feeds 15
30 minutes

- 100g caster sugar (6 heaped tablespoons)
- 250g butter
- 2 teaspoons vanilla essence
- 250g plain flour (18 heaped tablespoons)
- 2 baking trays

You can add a teaspoon of grated ginger, cinnamon or nutmeg for a festive flavour.

GO

1 Preheat the oven to 180°C/350°F/Gas Mark 4 and cover two baking trays with greaseproof paper.

2 Put the sugar, butter, vanilla essence and flour into a blender and blitz until the mixture becomes like breadcrumbs. Alternatively, follow steps 1–3 of the step-by-step instructions for how to 'rub in' the mixture by hand.

3 Tip the mixture back into the bowl and start to push down so that it forms a stiff ball of dough (see step 4). On a lightly floured surface or board, roll the dough out with a rolling pin (see steps 5 and 6) or push flat with the palm of your hand until it's about the same thickness as your thumb (1cm).

4 Use a cookie cutter or a knife to make shapes in the dough. You can make people, letters, stars – whatever you like! Then using a spatula, gently lift the biscuits and place on the baking trays.

5 Bake in the oven for 10–15 minutes or until very lightly golden. Sprinkle with sugar and leave to cool.

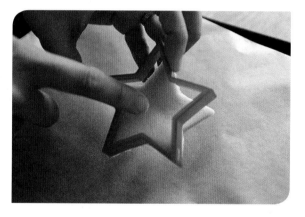

If you're allergic to eggs or just don't have any and fancy some comfort food, these bite-sized shortbread stars are really simple and taste lovely. They'll keep for 1-2 days in an airtight container and make a very cheap snack!

REWARD CHOCO-VANILLA PANCAKES

Feeds 2
20 minutes

GRAB

- 5 heaped tablespoons plain flour
- 2 eggs
- Pinch of salt
- ½ pint milk (use a pint glass to measure)
- 2 teaspoons vanilla extract
- 1 teaspoon drinking chocolate/hot chocolate powder
- Olive oil

Serve with ice cream, banana or fresh berries.

This recipe is a sweet reward for an exam victory. To reduce the calorie count you can replace the ice cream with a scoop of frozen yoghurt, it's just as yummy!

GO

1 Place the flour into a large bowl and make a well in the middle, scooping the flour out with the tablespoon.

2 Crack the eggs into the well, allowing them to fill it up, then add the salt. Whisk the eggs, gradually mixing in the flour and adding the milk. Add the vanilla extract. Stir in the chocolate powder until it is evenly distributed. Whisk the pancake mixture until smooth, then leave to stand for about 15 minutes.

3 Heat a splash of oil in a non-stick frying pan. When the oil begins to smoke, add about 3 tablespoons of the pancake mixture and swirl it round until the base of the pan is covered.

4 Cook until the edges start to crisp up and then gently use a spatula to lift up an edge. If the pancake comes away easily, it's time to flip it and cook the other side. When each pancake is fully cooked, place it on a plate. If the pan becomes dry, just add another splash of oil before adding more mixture.

5 Repeat the above until all the mixture is used up, then stack the pancakes to serve.

5
USEFUL RESOURCES

SAVING MONEY ON FOOD

Save 20% off food at railway stations!

‣ www.bitecard.co.uk

Like growing herbs, recycling peelings or thinking of sowing potatoes in a tyre?

‣ Check out *The Self Sufficient-ish Bible* by Andy Hamilton and Dave Hamilton (Hodder & Stoughton, 2008). It's a really great starting point for those who are fed up with high food bills.

‣ Visit www.lovefoodhatewaste.com for tips on how to save money on food, what to do with your waste and more.

Want to know how to get your five a day on the cheap?

‣ Check out www.nhs.uk/Livewell/5ADAY/Pages/Tencheapways.aspx

Student money-saving offers on food and more

‣ www.studentbeans.com

‣ www.savethestudent.org/save-money/food-drink

‣ www.thestudentroom.co.uk/wiki/Student_Food

FINDING ORGANIC FOOD

‣ *The Savvy Shopper* by Rose Prince (Fourth Estate, 2006) is an eye-opening and interesting read. Prince explores the most popular food issues and has lists of lots of places to get organic food.

‣ Places like supermarket aisles and farmers' markets are pretty good – especially when you get to talk to the stallholder and find out where your food is from!

INFORMATION ON FOOD INTOLERANCES AND ALLERGIES

Food intolerance in general

‣ www.bbc.co.uk/health/physical_health/conditions/foodintolerance1.shtml

Lactose intolerance

‣ www.nhs.uk/Conditions/lactose-intolerance/Pages/Treatment.aspx

Fructose intolerance

‣ http://en.wikipedia.org/wiki/Fructose_malabsorption

Coeliac disease

‣ www.nhs.uk/conditions/coeliac-disease
‣ Going gluten free: *Seriously Good! Gluten-Free Cooking* by Phil Vickery (in association with Coeliac UK; Kyle Cathie, 2009).
‣ *Living Gluten Free For Dummies* by Sue Baic, Nigel Denby and Danna Korn (John Wiley, 2007).
‣ www.bbc.co.uk/food/diets/gluten_free

Irritable Bowel Syndrome (IBS)

‣ *Irritable Bowel Solutions: The Essential Guide to IBS, Its Causes and Treatments* by Dr John Hunter (Vermilion, 2007; also in Kindle edition)
‣ www.nhs.uk/conditions/irritable-bowel-syndrome

Food allergies

‣ Check out www.allergyuk.org
‣ An awful lot of food contains nuts or is made around nuts these days, especially takeaways. A great book for those who have or think they have a nut allergy is *How to Live with a Nut Allergy: Everything You Need to Know If You Are Allergic to Peanuts or Tree Nuts* by Chad Oh and Carol Kennedy (McGraw-Hill, 2004; also in Kindle edition)

KEEPING A BALANCE

Body Mass Index

‣ www.nhs.uk/Tools/Pages/Healthyweightcalculator.aspx

Alcohol intake

‣ www.drinkaware.co.uk
‣ www.nhs.uk/Change4Life/Pages/understanding-alcohol.aspx

All about energy drinks

‣ http://science.howstuffworks.com/innovation/edible-innovations/energy-drink.htm

Eating disorders

‣ www.nhs.uk/Livewell/eatingdisorders

See it yourself

‣ www.channel4.com/programmes/tags/health-and-wellbeing – programmes from Channel 4 on real-life issues and lots of information on food- and nutrition-related questions.

INDEX